CONTENTS

© COPYRIGHT DONALD FORD 1995

DESIGN EDMONDS ADVERTISING

PUBLISHED IN 1995 BY DONALD FORD IMAGES,

6-7 HIGH STREET,

SOUTH QUEENSFERRY

EH30 9PP

A CIP CATALOGUE RECORD IS AVAILABLE FROM THE BRITISH LIBRARY

ISBN   0 9525124 0 8

FRONT COVER: AUTUMN SILHOUETTES, LINLITHGOW

BACK COVER: AUTUMN, SCOTT'S VIEW

INTRODUCTION

Donald Ford was born in Linlithgow in 1944, the younger son of Alec, local veterinary surgeon, and Betty, former legal secretary and Director of Red Cross in West Lothian. Donald followed in the sporting footsteps of his father (who in the 1920's, won three caps for Scotland at cricket), of elder brother Malcolm (seventeen caps), and of his mother, a low handicap member of Linlithgow Golf Club. Football came first, however.

By 1964, when he was half-way through his five-year indenture to an Edinburgh firm of Chartered Accountants, he had joined, as an amateur, Heart of Midlothian, after a season as a Junior with Bo'ness United.

He passed his C.A. finals in the summer of 1967 and, early in 1968, took two major decisions. The first was to sign professional forms for Hearts; the second was to open his own accounting practice in his home town. He subsequently enjoyed a further seven seasons at Tynecastle, not winning any honours with the club, but gaining three full Scottish caps in 1973/74. After one season with Falkirk, a knee ligament injury forced his retiral from the game.

His cricketing career continued apace, however, and in his third season as captain of West Lothian, he was included in the first-ever Scotland squad to compete for the Benson & Hedges Trophy in 1980. Mixing sporting metaphors, he "hit the cross bar" and never won the Scottish cricket Cap he would dearly have wished to place alongside those of his father and brother.

Professionally, he continued to practise in Linlithgow and then, from 1989, in Bathgate, but in 1990 he became totally disenchanted with the increasing pressures which were being brought to bear on sole practitioners. These were causing him increasing anxiety, and inevitably, a growing number of sleepless nights.

This book tells the story of his decision to abandon his career in Accountancy and the security which came with it. He graphically relates his subsequent leap into an unknown marketplace (for him at any rate) which he hoped would exist for his photographs of the Scottish landscape, blissfully unaware that in 1991 a severe recession was beginning to remove a great deal of disposable income from the pockets of his potential customers.

Donald honestly reveals his anxieties, his mistakes, disappointments and disasters, but also the complete and utter contentment he discovered in his new career. His love of, and empathy with, the magnificence of Scotland's chameleon countryside and seashore is revealed in some sixty pictures in a growing portfolio of highly acclaimed photographic compositions and moods.

He describes the preparations which are required before he embarks on a trip, and the excitement he has felt on several of those which were made into some parts of Scotland he had never before seen. He offers sound, if sometimes pointed, advice to the thousands of camera-toting amateurs who annually scour the country taking photographs.

He concludes with a look ahead, both for himself and for photography as a whole, and expresses the hope that he is not suddenly to waken and discover it has all been a dream.

BEE(CH) CRAIGS
This lovely shot of the avenue of beech trees at Beecraigs Country Park, between Bathgate and Linlithgow, was taken in steady rain and required a three second exposure as the light was very poor. The end result was worth the soaking.

THE END OF AN ERA

By the Spring of 1990, I knew that something would have to give. Inexorably, the practice had increased demands on my time, and as clients' problems required ever more attention, a ten - hour working day with the briefest, if any, break for lunch, became the norm'. Our evening meal would inevitably be followed by a sleep in an armchair and the predictable exhausted collapse into bed was sooner rather than later.

This was no way to live and while all sole owners have to make sacrifices, the potential damage to home life and total loss of time for leisure or recreation was a price which was just too high to pay.

What was most disturbing, however, was the growing habit of my awakening in the small hours of the morning. Instantly, as if the alarm clock had sounded four hours early, my mind was off and running. Within minutes a multifarious collection of client problems, taxation queries, growing backlogs of correspondence or forthcoming meetings had ensured that no further rest was enjoyed that night.

It *is* worse at night, too. Somehow, in the darkness, the problems are insoluble. When you close your eyes you don't find a way out, and anxiety builds on anxiety until the whole thing is a nightmare. Morning is merciful in its arrival as it allows you to *do* something to ease the worrying. The pale, drawn face and bags under the eyes said it all.

At this point I had to stop and take stock. My wife Carol, who incidentally, is the best unpaid analyst of peoples' minds I have ever met, did not require to call on her skills in this direction to offer a solution, because it was really staring me in the face. The options, she reckoned, were either a nervous breakdown within a year or a heart attack anytime. If I recall correctly, she put it a bit more bluntly (Leithers are like that, I understand) and used her favourite description of me - 'you're running around like a ferret - disappearing up your own back-end!' - to emphasise her point.

So it all had to change. Having, in 1982, retired from my original practice in Linlithgow, then a four-partner concern, I had no wish to examine the acquisition of partners again. I am not, obviously, a great 'partner' person.

To be honest, as the late 1980's saw the introduction of huge chunks of legislation (tighter V.A.T. controls, the Financial Services Act, and far reaching auditing requirements for small companies,) it had become obvious that some additional qualified assistance was going to be essential in the practice. That anxiety, and the huge rise in fees to clients which would inevitably follow, was just another avenue for a racing mind to explore at three o'clock in the morning.

I dismissed also the possibility of an amalgamation, perhaps with a larger Edinburgh firm, as I wished to protect the aspect of individual attention which I had tried to give each client. Partners in bigger firms tend not to have time for that or have insufficient business management or communications skills to do it well. Alternatively they charge gigantic fees for consultations so that the client is dissuaded from asking for advice again.

That left one option - a sale of the practice as a going concern. I wondered whether other sole practitioners or small partnerships with similar ideals to my own were around and I explored this possibility with Alasdair Young, who was in charge of Members' Services at our Institute in Edinburgh. Despite a few hiccups, his help and encouragement had allowed me by the end of 1990, to negotiate a disposal of the practice to the satisfaction of all parties concerned. Clients and staff, at this point, had absolutely no idea of what lay ahead.

I needed then to take a deep breath, talk things over again with Carol and come to a final decision. To be honest, as sleepless night had followed sleepless night, it wasn't difficult. Nevertheless I had no little torment.

AFTERGLOW
You always keep your tripod legs crossed when a promising sunset is in the offing, but this was a stunner, and in four years I have never seen another like it. The sun has just dipped behind the Ochils and lights the clouds from below. The shot was taken with a zoom lens from the Bathgate Hills and required metering from the orange clouds to catch the image the way I wanted it.

Twelve years of solid education in Linlithgow had been followed by five years of a C.A. apprenticeship in Edinburgh. Indentured to a five-partner practice I had learned everything I knew about the theory of accounting, auditing and taxation. Long Friday night and Saturday morning classes, heavy hours of swatting for exams and worries about passing or failing ultimately paid off with my getting through my Finals in the summer of 1967.

Twenty three years of private practice had followed thereafter, during which I built up two thriving businesses. Was it right - or logical - that I should throw forty years away? I fully understood that, once out of the firm and away from the constant up-dating on new legislation, tax planning and other essential ingredients of maintaining and improving services to clients, there would, and could, be no return. Certainly there were

some opportunities in my field which might be available. More than a few clients, when ultimately learning of the retiral, mentioned the possibility of my helping them out at a future date if circumstances were right. I am pleased, in one instance so far, that has been fruitful. Basically, however, at the age of forty six I was fully aware that retiral from practice then meant retiral from practice forever.

In the continuing helter-skelter of modern business, with pressures building up all around,and with two thirds of my allotted 'three score and ten' behind me I wanted to enjoy life again; to sleep comfortably, to be a better companion to Carol and to find a way to make a living where money was not the be-all and end-all but where quality of life could still be recognised and attained. The decision was really straight forward, with no shades of grey. I would sell the practice.

The question of what would come next was again answered by Carol before I even raised it. Christmas 1986 had seen the gift of a new camera from her. Photography had been a hobby for a long number of years, and the outfit which I had bought in the late 60's (a Practika 35mm body with standard lens and 135mm telephoto) was beginning to show its age, although I had some tremendous results from it and was very sad to see it go.

The Minolta 7000 with which she presented me was at that time the state- of -the-art camera. It was the first fully-automatic model and any of four modes could be used for picture taking. If you were not a creative photographer, for example, you could leave the camera set in programme mode and it would do everything for you except press the shutter!

In the years which followed, my landscape photography was elevated to a plane which surprised me. I did appear to have an eye for composition, I saw things around me which produced pleasing images and, while still very much a hobby my overall picture-taking came on in leaps and bounds.

By the time we sat down in 1990 to discuss my future, one avenue was obvious. 'Why don't you have a go at landscape photography as a career?' she asked. 'Could you make something out of it?', "At least you would enjoy what you were doing". I didn't need a second chance. I had always loved the Scottish landscape, from the days when my father, time permitting, would take me around the Trossachs or into Perthshire, Fife, The Borders and - on our annual holidays in Carnoustie - into the Angus Glens. Then throughout school days when geography - especially of Scotland - was a favourite subject; and finally in the sixties and seventies, travelling around the country playing cricket and football, and finding out even from train or coach windows what an astonishing landscape is around us.

The idea in one sense seemed too good to be true. While the successful disposal of the practice, on paper, would ensure that we would be financially secure for some eighteen months or so, I had that time span to build income from another source. I got to work on some figures and reckoned - all things being equal - that I could earn sufficient profit from sales of photographs to make it all work. Every forecast I used of course was produced from nothing more than intelligent guess work as I had no comparisons or previous knowledge to build upon (and how could I possibly have forecast that Britain was on the verge of a brutal recession?).

The manner in which I would market my work, however, was in hind- sight dismissed far too quickly and as things turned out (even allowing for the recession) wildly optimistic. Although hind -sight is a wonderful thing it is totally useless in forecasting, and the prospects were sufficiently encouraging to persuade (without, I have to admit, too much difficulty) another courageous Scorpio to take the plunge.

And so the deed was done. Final meetings were held with the two purchasers of the practice (an east/west split of clients was ultimately agreed as there were too many for one simplified takeover). Letters of offer were exchanged and 6th April, 1991 arranged as the date of takeover.

Much had to be done meantime. Again in retrospect while I would never have changed the decision I made I could *never* go through two months again like February and March of that year. The pressures were horrific despite my looking forward to the release from worry and the prospect of an exciting new career. The days were filled with one meeting after another, explanations and words of comfort to clients that they would be well looked after by my successors.

Most traumatic of all, without a doubt, were the efforts to allay the fears of members of staff who, over the previous three or four years had helped me to build the practice, and who were suddenly to learn that their employer, out of the blue, was on the face of it leaving them afloat on pretty stormy waters. Even their place of work would shift too, as my premises were not required by either firm involved in the practice takeover.

I will never forget the morning I called them together to break the news. I had

LAST CAST
Regrettably not a west coast sunset but one from our Spanish holidays in La Manga. Unbelievable cloud formations and the availability of a convenient fisherman provided all that was required.

rehearsed, for days, how I would phrase the announcement. Then how I would confidently talk to each individually, to discuss fears they might have and answer questions on their roles in the new situation. Needless to say it turned out vastly different to the rehearsals.

I knew that morning would be traumatic but I probably underestimated the effect by around two hundred percent and, without going into detail, I hope I am never placed in a position again where such a bombshell can cause so much anxiety and upset to people who don't deserve it. It must have been awful for them.

Nevertheless, the Rubicon had been crossed and plans had to be followed up. Countless meetings with clients, bank managers and other business associates followed over the eight weeks or so until the date of sale. The vast majority of clients, while

SNOWY MORNING, BEECRAIGS
An overnight dusting of snow, a little winter sunlight, and a nice composition can make a fairly ordinary scene a stunning picture. Taken at right angles to the autumn shot which came along ten months later.

sympathetic and totally understanding.

I hoped that I had chosen my successors wisely and that they would subsequently handle clients just as efficiently and attentively as in the past. In fact the way things were heading, the probability had existed that some dilution of the personal service they had previously enjoyed was going to be inevitable. I simply wasn't coping with the situation anyway.

Clients were extremely supportive although a few disappointments lay ahead as some decided not to follow the practice into new hands to give them an opportunity to see what my successors could do, and they switched to other firms instead. I had anticipated some reaction but was disappointed in a few instances by clients who moved swiftly to other practices. Of course it was entirely their prerogative.

The doors officially closed, therefore, on Monday, 6th April, 1991. Furniture, equipment, fittings and files were all removed to their new homes in a welter of activity in the next day or two and, incredibly quickly it seemed, a bustling, noisy office was quiet and empty.

Nevertheless I had absolutely no regrets. The relief of pressure (this horribly over- used word in today's world) was evident immediately and that far outweighed, as I suspected it would, the loss of a career built up over a large number of years.

I had learned, perhaps ten or twelve years before, that looking back on life was a recipe for nothing but negativity. What was done was done, and could never be restored or renewed. Dwelling on the past therefore was simply a non-starter. Besides, there was a new career ahead, the planning and organisation of which could now proceed at full speed. I would also be doing it free from worry and fresh from a decent night's sleep. I cannot overestimate just how good that felt.

A NEW CAREER

"Whatever you can do, or dream you can, begin it,
Boldness has genius and magic in it."
(Goethe)

THE HARBOUR, CRAIL
The householders around Crail harbour must be sick of artists and photographers, and who can blame them? This is a favourite shot from my first visit. A few lobster pots, a handily placed moored yacht, the tide, at just the right stage, and a different picture of Crail resulted.

For Christmas 1986, Carol gifted me a brand new Minolta 7000 SLR camera, complete with standard 50mm lens and flash gun. While obviously excited about the possibilities which this new 'state of the art' camera could generate, there was more than a tinge of sadness as I parted with my Praktica which, despite its years, had produced some quality photographs. It was bought by a gentleman from Livingston for his son, who was showing some encouraging results from his photography - I often wonder if it helped him to develop a career.

In the four years or so which followed, I discovered that my picture taking had certainly reached a new level; the images were the sharpest I had ever seen and the camera's own excellence was a spur in itself to obtaining a better shot each time I went out with it. Regrettably this was only when work permitted, or on our annual holidays to La Manga in Spain where I captured some spectacular sunsets. They still feature as some of the best and most memorable shots in the portfolio.

There was a great temptation, in the early days, to allow the camera to take everything in 'Programme' mode. Minolta were the first manufacturers to bring a fully auto-focusing computerised camera to the market place. In attempting to take shots in difficult lighting situations, particularly where there were lighter or darker backgrounds to subjects, the camera's meter simply couldn't cope and I finished up with grey photographs which were neither one thing nor the other and inevitably went in the bucket!

I began experimenting with, first of all, 'Manual' mode - in other words setting everything myself and ignoring what the camera was telling me to do. Having purchased a cheap exposure meter to compare readings from it with the camera's meter I began to create the images I was looking for and in particular some stunning sunset-silhouette shots from around the West Lothian countryside.

It is probably six or seven years since I last used 'Programme' mode to take a picture on the Minolta: I invariably set a small aperture of F16, F19 or F22 and I have grown so used to the outstanding qualities of Fuji Reala that I know I will be shooting at, almost without exception, a quarter, an eighth or a fifteenth of a second at F22 - obviously depending on the lighting conditions.

Nine years later, the results from the camera are still absolutely outstanding. The message, however, is clear; if you want to create your own pictures then don't become a slave to the new "all singing and dancing" cameras which will do everything for you. Improvements there have obviously been in metering and associated characteristics by the leading camera manufacturers but you will certainly lose some outstanding picture possibilities if you rely totally on the mechanics to do the job for you.

AMULREE KIRK
Much photographed, but rarely from this angle (the little road to Glen Quaich). I thought the inclusion of the fence and the rough grass emphasised the comparative remoteness of the kirk; hence its position top right.

By the time I was packing up the practice, I had, perhaps, some twenty or thirty pictures which were of exhibitable and, hopefully, saleable quality. I estimated that I needed at least one hundred pictures before I presented to them the public and so my first priority was to identify areas of the country which would allow the addition of some sixty or seventy pictures to the current stock.

While I was deliberating where my first shoot should be, the matter was decided for me by a friend whose family belonged to Lower Largo in Fife. It was a place I had never visited but when he talked about the sea-front houses, the beach, the viaduct and the estuary of the burn, it sounded absolutely ideal. Thus photographic expedition number one was decided upon and a suitable early morning weather report all that was required.

By this time my camera equipment had expanded to include a 70 - 210 zoom lens and an assortment of filters plus the essential tripod (any serious photographer simply cannot do without one). A few mornings later, I hardly needed the alarm (not having slept a wink all night through excitement!). It duly went off at 5.30am, woke the entire household, and within half an hour I was on the road to Fife along with camera gear, maps, coffee and sandwiches (another essential part of the equipment!).

Sunrise in the middle of April is around 7 am, but I had no worries about reaching Lower Largo before the sun came up as a broad belt of unbroken cloud killed any lightness that may have been in the early morning sky.

I simply didn't believe that the weather forecasters could be that far out but, having arrived at Lower Largo in time to hear the latest forecast just before the 7 am news, I was encouraged to learn that the cloud which had gathered overnight (and which hadn't been mentioned on the forecast the night before!) was expected to clear by mid-day.

As if that wasn't enough, Fife Regional Council had been sufficiently inconsiderate to decide to renew the main sewer along the sea-front. The workmen duly arrived around 8am and within minutes the promenade was awash with JCB's and heavy lorries. The anticipated pictures of pretty sea-front cottages promptly disappeared.

I gave it until 9am, went for a wander along the beach and took a few photographs of the rock formations, pools and seaweed, and with not the slightest evidence of any chink in the mass of grey above, decided to call it a day, headed for home and got the drawing board out again. It was a bad start but things could only improve. They did - a week or so later.

No serious photographer, in my opinion, should be without the 'Walk Scotland' series of books published by Bartholomews. Covering most parts of the country which walkers and visitors would like to explore, they give invaluable and detailed descriptions of routes, terrain and recommendations on protective clothing and footwear. Most important of all from a photographer's point of view are the descriptions of outstanding viewpoints along the way.

I invested my first £3.95 in the edition covering Fife, the Lothians and the Borders and, still in search of an elusive sunrise, decided that my next trip would be to the Berwickshire coast and an exploration of Fast Castle, a virtual ruin perched precariously on a cliff-top a few miles north of St. Abbs.

It was another 5am rise and as the A1 turned me southwards at Dunbar, the skies to the east were already lightening and the promise of a fine sunrise had me more than a little excited.

At that time of the morning, the roads were empty and I was in the car park roughly a mile from the cliff-top in good time to catch the rising sun - if it eventually appeared.

The directions in the handbook for this particular exploration of the Berwickshire coast were first class. Unfortunately the narrative didn't mention anything about a biting wind blowing off the North Sea, which threatened at times to whip my contact lenses out. It was still April of course, and it was absolutely freezing. However, within fifteen minutes I was in sight of the ruins and it is pretty difficult to put into words the excitement I felt despite the utter isolation of it all.

The wind was bitter and it fairly threw the waves against the cliffs a hundred feet below me. Whoever had the idea to build a stronghold on this remote outcrop hundreds of years ago must surely have had a screw loose, or was terribly desperate. Although really there are only a few piles of bricks left here and there, (obviously, it wasn't one of Wallace Mercer's developments) it was not hard to imagine the inaccessibility of the castle, or similarly the ease with which it ought to have been defended. (For reading enthusiasts, by the way, Sir Walter Scott used the castle in his novel 'The Bride of Lammermoor'. He called it 'Wolf's Crag.')

Eventually dawn broke, the sun rose; alas, not gloriously, but hazily behind a thin veil of morning cloud. There were picture opportunities, however, and I made the most of it.

One shot in particular, of the castle and the Wheat Stack, with the early morning sun glinting off the waves, is still a favourite photograph, perhaps because it was my first real capture, but also because I think I caught the mood of the place in the prevailing conditions.

I had hoped to get further shots of the cliffs, the sea birds which frequent this part of Berwickshire (and anything else that took my fancy because there is always the unexpected in photography) but the layer of cloud began to thicken and I packed up and made my way back up the hillside to the car. Admittedly, this time, I had a feeling of exhilaration and anticipation of seeing some positive results from my early morning adventure.

In fact, the morning got better and better. I drove the five miles or so to St. Abbs and took a few shots round one of Scotland's loveliest little harbours, now much frequented by scuba-divers. While the hustle and bustle of the village's former fishing

REEDS, LILIES AND BOAT, LOCHARD
A wonderful picture and a perfect example of the stroke of luck. Not brilliant light, but an absolutely fabulous composition and colour balance among all the greens, with the flash of the little boat an ideal, and contrasting, focal point.

trade has now passed a few miles down the coast to its neighbour Eyemouth, there is still activity in the harbour and the atmosphere still draws hundreds of tourists, artists and photographers every year.

[Space does not permit me to describe in detail a 1994 trip to the area; suffice to say that I spent one and a half hours on the cliffs just north of the village waiting for a bank of cloud to blow over; the wait was well worth it as a super shot of a weird rock pillar framing the village rewarded my patience.]

Incidentally, the walk from the car park at Northfield Farm to the cliffs, then past the lighthouse and on towards Fast Castle is one of the classic cliff-top walks in Scotland. In summertime it is accompanied by a crescendo of noise as the huge adult sea-bird population struggles manfully to maintain its flow of food to thousands of the young

families perched on the cliff-face anywhere that they can find a space! (Having made it safely back to Northfield Farm, by the way, the home baking is something else!)

The Berwickshire trip was given an unexpected bonus on the return journey when I took the advice of the walking guide and stopped at Tyninghame, midway between Dunbar and North Berwick, had a lovely walk with the camera through the woods and emerged onto the superb sandy beach to the north of the Tyne Estuary. The Bass Rock, perhaps four miles away, was a little hazy in the morning sunshine but one photograph of the sands taken from the dunes above the beach is still proving an excellent seller for me. This is a glorious stretch of unspoiled sand for those of either a recreational or artistic bent and, given the right light, the seascapes are stunning.

The Fast Castle trip, therefore, is especially etched in my memory. Not only did it overcome the disaster of the previous week at Lower Largo, it created six or eight additions to my portfolio, and not a few surprises as well. Leaving aside the benefits of the physical exercise in walking almost four miles, I began to feel very excited at the prospect of future trips around the country proving as lucrative as this one from a photographic point of view, and also of the enjoyment of a country which has to be the most beautiful in the world.

TWILIGHT, FORTH BRIDGE
Captured thousands of times by camera enthusiasts since Prince Edward switched the lights on, my version was taken from a different location (sorry - it's a secret!) and I used a blue filter to correct any colour cast from the lighting. I think it adds to the coolness of the evening on which it was taken.

Running along-side the quandary surrounding where on earth I should start taking pictures was the other obvious question of where I should test the market.

N ot having nearly enough stuff to open a retail outlet in a High Street anywhere and in the absence of confirmation that the public would eventually buy what I was producing, I felt that the only solution was to take the material to the people rather than waiting for the people to come to see the goods. I decided, after some deliberation, to design a mobile gallery which I could take to agricultural shows, horse trials, game fairs etc. around the country. Provided it was nicely fitted-out inside and had good lighting, I thought it would be an excellent vehicle for the purpose required. After a couple of meetings with coach builders in Falkirk (and more than a few rubbings out and alterations to my original design) an order was placed and delivery of the trailer promised for May - just in time for the range of out-door summer events around Scotland.

All I had to do now was to sell the pictures. How simple or difficult that would prove to be I would soon know as I had booked my first show for the summer, the International Carriage Driving Championships at Drumlanrig Castle, near Dumfries.

It was a two-day event, with setting up on Friday. My younger son, Alistair, had bravely volunteered to help me out and, having hitched up the mobile gallery to the rear of the Subaru, we headed off down the A70.

I had absolutely no idea that the weight and 'squareness' of the gallery would cause so much gear-changing and it took far longer to reach our destination than I had imagined. While we didn't have any hairy moments on the trip, Alistair's main enjoyment was counting the number of vehicles in the convoys which regularly piled up in our wake, especially on the A702 between Crawford and Thornhill, with Dalveen Pass, in particular, being an absolute nightmare.

Incessant rain which had been falling all day simply compounded the difficulties and when we eventually made it to Drumlanrig the normally beautiful grounds were, simply, a

EVENING SUN, OBAN
The "usual" shot of the town, harbour, and McCaig's Folly overlooking the scene. Lovely April afternoon sunlight picks out the colour mix among the boats.

PRINCES STREET GARDENS
The very heart of Scotland's capital, captured from
Princes Street Gardens on a lovely autumn morning.

swamp. Tractors, oil skinned stewards and chaos were everywhere. Having been directed towards our stance by one of those in charge, it took less than a minute for us to be stuck fast in approximately two feet of clinging mud. Four-wheel drive is a wonderful thing, but even it cannot cope with conditions such as these, and it took the arrival of a tractor some ten minutes later to pull us clear. Eventually - not without a feeling of great relief - I had manoeuvred in to our space and unhooked the gallery. It was a much easier journey home!

To say that I was nervous on the Saturday morning, when we arrived back at Drumlanrig and opened up the gallery, would be the understatement of the year. I was terrified. I had absolutely no idea what the reaction of the public would be, and whether I could sell anything or not, but, some thirty six hours later, I had a few answers.

Total takings for the weekend amounted to £69, which after a deduction for stand rent, petrol, lunches etc. produced a net loss of £40. While that was disappointing there *were* positives. The people who saw my pictures liked them - it was unfortunate that only a few of them bought them! I learned, in competition with a lot of other traders at the Show, that I simply could not expect the public to prefer my goods to those of others, which were less of a luxury than a picture to hang on the wall. Although I didn't know it at the time, it was obvious that the recession was biting hard and people simply weren't prepared to spend the money which they might have in the boom of the late 1980's.

The Drumlanrig experience was repeated at many other shows which I did in 1991 and 1992; Thirlestane Castle, Blair Atholl, Coupar Angus, Kelso and Perth were all locations where organised events, despite fairly good attendances, yielded little profit - and often further net losses - despite positive, and generally laudatory, comments on the quality of my material.

Similarly, exhibitions of my own which I had scheduled in Kelso, Stirling, Aberfoyle, Glenrothes, Callander and Anstruther, were equally disappointing in terms of turnover. The exhibition at Anstruther was, perhaps, the lowest point of my first two years.

I knew the area well and in particular the business of the Craw's Nest Hotel in the town. The Birrell family, who run it superbly, could not have been more helpful when I suggested that I might organise an exhibition of my pictures one Sunday. I had, already, a strong collection of East Neuk of Fife photographs and I was genuinely optimistic that things would turn out well.

I had spent heavily on advertising in the two weeks leading up to the event, and the fact that I had persuaded the whole family - Carol, Lee, Campbell and Alistair - to lend their support was an indication of the confidence which I had in the likely success of the exhibition.

The attendance of members of the family was swelled unexpectedly by the arrival of Carol's brother Tony and his two daughters from North Wales and there were therefore nine members of the Ford and Crerar family present when we completed preparations and opened the doors around twelve noon that Sunday.

It was an absolute disaster. The lunchtime business in the hotel, as usual, was excellent but few of the customers ventured through to inspect my work. Those who did seemed genuinely taken with the quality of the photography but, again, there were few sales.

That Sunday afternoon was probably the lowest point I had reached since beginning the new business, and the gloom was only lifted by a most enjoyable evening meal which we all had in Anstruther before heading home.

Hindsight as we all know, is a wonderful thing, but, practically, is of absolutely no use to man nor beast. Stand up, yours truly, as yet another example of one on whom this realisation dawned some eighteen months after the beginning of the business.

There is absolutely no doubt in my mind that, of all the planning and forecasting and researching and questioning and changing of direction which had all been part of my preparation to leap off the cliff in 1991, the area of marketing, which was least known to me, was dismissed far too lightly. I never asked myself "what if framed pictures don't sell?" or "what if framed pictures sell but not in sufficient quantity or at the price levels I anticipate?" or "apart from the general public, what other type of people might like to buy my photographs?". So it was , when it became obvious that the quality of the work was adequate, but the volume of sales was not, that thinking caps suddenly had to be donned, and avenues explored which hopefully would yield good new connections and, in the future, bits and pieces of additional income.

I describe later my school homework on cold selling of my greeting cards, which Carol tried hard to impart in the winter of 1993. What has not yet been recounted, however, are two other main aspects of marketing which I attempted, the first of which, in the autumn of 1991 was an abject failure, the second of which, despite causing great frustrations and not a little annoyance, brought some positive results.

I had known Alan Wilson, Financial Controller of Radio Forth, for many years,

AUTUMN IN KELVINGROVE
One of three lovely November pictures taken in Kelvingrove with a new Agfa film I was trying out. Stunning colours and just a bit of the famous landmark as a contrast

following a connection which we had built up at the birth of the station in the mid-1970's. Despite the enormity of the workload before him, a lot of which demands the highest priority, he has always regularly and unselfishly found ten minutes when I dropped in to see him for a blether.

With the connection to a large number of Advertising Agencies across the central belt of Scotland, it was his suggestion that I should try to meet with the Creative Directors of those who might regularly be seeking Scottish landscapes for corporate brochures, exhibitions and the like.

Armed with my list of Edinburgh and Glasgow Agencies, therefore, I spent a morning on the telephone arranging appointments where I could, concentrating on Edinburgh first of all to see how I would get on.

Over the next couple of weeks, I subsequently had some eight or ten meetings, approaching each with mixed feelings (rather like the young lad who watched his new sports car going over a cliff with his mother-in-law at the wheel!). Obviously, I had great anticipation but also was understandably nervous at the reception which the samples of my photography would receive.

On the whole I was courteously welcomed but by the conclusion of my third visit, had reached the depressing conclusion that I would not derive any business from the connections. Almost without exception, the Agencies were demanding medium or large format photographs, which obviously I could not supply at the time as all my work was in 35mm. Despite my assurances that extremely sharp prints as large as 4' x 3' had been produced from my work, there was a pretty universal demand that prints or transparencies should be of a larger format to ensure maximum sharpness when published. (In retrospect, I find that remark difficult to swallow when a large proportion of published photographs finish up no larger than 3" x 2", and sometimes smaller!).

Despite the disappointment which I felt at the time, I was getting some valuable advice, and I pursued the other meetings over the next couple of weeks, generally with the same result although it was nice to hear from people in the Advertising Industry. who were demanding such high standards, that in the main they liked the look of my work and could be well be inclined to call on me in the future, assuming the format was upgraded. At the time of writing, some three years later, I have supplied three Agencies with photographs.

Putting Edmonds Advertising (who, as the reader will know from another chapter have been a tremendous encouragement to me since I began my new career) on one side, neither of the other two had met me before but had picked up my name from a handbook of Scottish photographers in which I had made another investment of several hundred pounds. That was another marketing attempt which is yet to bring any tangible returns.

Happily, some business has been done with another connection which I made in the autumn of 1991. By that time, I had some 150 photographs in the portfolio and felt sufficiently confident of the quality of the majority to launch myself on a few unsuspecting picture libraries. My first enquiry was to the Scottish Tourist Board, where a lady explained that a recent reconstruction of the Board's activities had resulted in the picture library being bought out privately but she was kind enough to give me the new telephone number and contact, so that I might take things further.

I was delighted that I did, because, as a result, I have met two delightful people, who, like myself, had taken the plunge into the big bad world of running their own business and, more importantly, had obviously risked a great deal of money in doing so. John Hutchison and Sue Hall set up the Still Moving Picture Library in the Logiegreen area of Edinburgh with the former Tourist Board's stock of some 30,000 transparencies as their initial stock in trade. I didn't believe for one moment that they would increase that to 30,150 by the automatic addition of what I had to offer, but arrived at their office armed with thirty or forty 12" x 8" prints to see what they thought of this new young photographer's work.

In fact, they seemed highly impressed but just as I was getting very excited at the prospect of some kind of dripping roast at last being being created, they asked if I had any transparencies, rather than prints. Having used negative, rather than reversal film for the vast majority of my photography to date, I had a minimum of slides to offer but they were good enough on my next visit, to retain some twelve or fifteen of these and while they made it quite clear in a salutary warning that I should expect no financial bonanza from such a small investment in the library, I was happy to get in on the ground floor and see what would develop in time to come.

Main marketing avenues, however continue to arise by taking my work to the people. With this original fundamental still very much in mind, a comment from a neighbouring stall holder at one of the craft fairs, which I did in 1992, resulted in my taking a stand at the Annual Trade Fair in Aviemore in October of that year. The four day show required an outlay of some £600 (including B&B, travelling expenses and of course the stand rental) but of course with thousands of Buyers from not only the U.K. but abroad visiting the show, I had high hopes that I would come back with a fair number of new outlets.

As you will see from the next chapter, I returned home for two days as Carol was unwell. Nick and Rosie Kerr ably handled any inquiries and contacts which were made in those two days, however, and while some new business did develop from the Show, on the whole I was disappointed that there had not been more enquiries.

There are, to be fair, hundreds upon hundreds of absolutely splendid Scottish-made Crafts to be seen at the Aviemore Trade Fair with, I grant you, many different traders displaying the same type of goods. (There were, for example, six landscape photographers at Aviemore in 1993). Therefore there must be disappointments but I cannot believe for a moment that perceptive or experienced Buyers disregard invitations to view at no cost, except for a few minutes of their time, a new potential supply line which might make money for their company.

Now that I have got that off my chest, can I also say that, in the brief moments I had at Aviemore to have a look round the whole show, it is incomprehensible that this country should ever have a Balance of Trade problem with the rest of the world. The quality of craftsmanship, invention and manufacture of hundreds upon hundreds of small traders "doing their own thing" across Scotland ought to be bringing a bonanza of exports to this country. It can only be because we are not marketing our goods abroad in the right fashion that this is not so. I am utterly convinced, especially since I have my own first hand experience now, that if the selling of Scottish-made goods was in the right hands, this country would never have to worry where revenues from North Sea Oil went since we would sustain the country through the rising sales of all the aforementioned "made in Scotland" products.

As I concluded on a previous page, I have no doubt that I completely underestimated the importance of marketing when I launched my new career. I believe that, if many small businessmen like myself were honest, they would likewise admit to such a short coming. Of course, it all needs money and it needs an acquired knowledge of the potential marketplace by experts. Perhaps, just at this point in time, there aren't many around who meet these requirements and that, therefore, it is a fact of life we will have to accept.

SUNSET AT CRAIGFORTH
All the colours in the spectrum show up in this stunning silhouette of two lonely trees growing out of the banks of the Forth, a mile west of Stirling. A lot of research had been done, a lot of patience was needed and, as often before, a stroke of luck with the light finished it off.

AUGUST IN THE PENTLANDS
Loganlea Reservoir and the Kips are the characters in this composition, but the heather steals the show.

By the summer of 1992 I had realised that a critical point had been reached. I could not throw any more money at the new business - I had exhausted any capital which had become available from the sale of the practice. Unless I could produce some reasonable signs of income over the next few months, I was aware that I would have to give serious consideration to packing it in and beginning the search for a new job. Before that unenviable prospect became reality, however, I had to put my thinking cap on again. Fortunately, I had one flash of inspiration and two strokes of luck!

The smallest framed picture which I sold consisted of a 3" by 2" photograph mounted in a little 'mini-clip' frame and, with a selling price of some £3.00, was highly popular with customers. With my marketing hat on, it suddenly dawned on me that, if the current market place was not interested in framed pictures from £12.00 upwards (which I had previously hoped would be my principle earner) then perhaps I should be targeting a much lower level and looking at volume sales of my photographs in a cheaper form. The fact that people had continued to admire my work convinced me that it would sell, provided I could find the right medium and the right price, and a complete stroke of luck in Edinburgh in June, 1992 provided the answer.

I was in an art shop to buy some odds and ends when I noticed they had a little pack of blank greeting cards for sale, on which artists could paint or draw their own compositions and then post them off in envelopes which were also supplied. I guessed that the cards where about the size required to fit my smallest photograph and I bought a pack of ten.

In stock, I already had some twenty or thirty of my exhibits published as 'mini-photos' and I put a few on the cards when I got home and showed them to Carol. She was taken by them and so, some three weeks later, I had a supply of them at the Royal Highland Show and they sold well.

The four day Show was an expensive one, an exhausting one, and not without its problems, notably the presence nearby of a competing marquee of English traders who were occupying a much more favoured position on the showground than those of us in 'Crafts From Scotland' All things considered however, the 1992 Highland Show was a turning point for me. Unquestionably, the availability of the greeting cards - now produced in two sizes - has provided an excellent base for the business.

Despite tremendous competition and a seemingly unending stream of new products within the range of cards available to the general public, a growing number of outlets across Scotland are selling mine. People like the local views and compositions, and also the fact that they are buying a real photograph on every card rather than a print - and the price isn't bad either!

So a stroke of luck had created an opportunity which Carol persuaded me to develop in a 'sales run' during the winter of 1993 but in the meantime another lucky break was to play an important part in further broadening the base of the business and in expanding the range of photography which I could bring to the market place.

While in practice, one of my major Edinburgh clients was Edmonds Advertising Ltd., an Advertising Agency based in Leith and for whom, from the Autumn of 1992, I had been continuing to do a bit of accounting consultancy work. The encouragement, advice and enthusiasm which Colin McLaren and his wife Marion in particular, and the rest of the staff as a whole, have given me in the last two or three years has been invaluable. On this particular visit, however, it was a throwaway remark by Marion (who looks after all client advertising for the company) which led to the next door opening for me.

She casually threw a copy of "Scotland - Home of Golf" - across her desk at me

MORNING AT SOCIETY
5am in the morning at a local picnic spot a mile west of South Queensferry. A different picture of the two bridges using the trees and a graduated filter - to complete a moody but very popular addition to the portfolio.

BOAT ON LOCH AILORT
The shoreline and sea-lochs from Ardnamurchan to Mallaig contain
some lovely stretches of white sand which produce great seascapes but
also help to create fantastic watercolours when the light is right. Thus
this shot of sun on the water and storm clouds in the background
- with the addition of the white boat - make a dramatic composition.

and suggested that I might be interested in having a look at the photographs. I did, and I also read the editorial and, having already collected some twenty or thirty of my own golf course photographs, I wondered if it might be worth approaching Pastime Publications Ltd - publishers of the annual handbook - to see if they might consider using my photography for the next edition.

Within five minutes, Marion had telephoned the Managing Director and I had an appointment to see him. Barrie Anderson was his name, he was immediately taken by the golf course pictures which I showed him and my excitement rose considerably when he asked me if I would consider doing the editorial for the handbook as well as the photography.

Having turned the possibilities over in my mind within the next forty eight hours, I confirmed to him that I would love to do both and we arranged to meet again in the New Year to discuss the arrangements for the 1994 publication. With a lot of help from some golfing colleagues, notably John Chillas, Jim Farmer, David Huish, Bernard Gallacher and a lot of input from Dougie Donnelly, my editorial and photographs duly appeared in the 1994 edition and, from all accounts, they were very well received. The 1995 publication is just off the press, and I believe is also going well.

Pastime Publications have also taken over the production of a corresponding handbook for England, for which, again, I was delighted to be invited to produce photographs and editorial. That offer produced a hectic, but most enjoyable, two months or so of trips south of the Border but the finished product went down well and it appears likely that I will be engaged again for next years publication. The major part of the editorial was contributed by Dalmahoy Pro, Andy Oldcorn, whose input and knowledge of English courses proved invaluable. What a delightful young man - and a credit to his profession. His love of Heart of Midlothian is just a bonus!

Quite suddenly, therefore, the closing months of 1992 yielded two new opportunities and, while the popping of champagne corks was a little premature, to say the least, I now had clear grounds for genuine optimism.

They were greatly increased by my encounter at the Aviemore Trade Fair with Andrew McKenna, himself a superb photographer but for whom the majority of a working day is spent widening the sales of his Fort William company, the Scottish Collection.

Andy also was taken by my photographs and, in particular, the golf course shots.

Consequently, four photographs appeared in the 1993 calendar and a repeat order for 1994 - this time with additional shots - presented me with the opportunity for another outlet for my work. The calendar market - like that of greeting cards - is fierce, and there are many photographers who would give their right arm to be presented with the opportunity which Andy has given me over the last couple of years.

In another chapter, I spend a little more time on the photography of the golf course, but I will always be grateful to this delightful young man for opening a door to me just when I needed it. For their part, Andy and his colleagues in Fort William have firmly established The Scottish Collection in the market place and they deserve to reap all the rewards which their excellent work and quality reproduction deserves.

The Aviemore Show was not an easy time. I was away from home for four long days and nights - at any rate I ought to have been - but Carol became unwell at home and I had to leave the show and travel back to West Calder. Fortunately, my 'neighbours' at Aviemore, Nik and Rosie Kerr, from Nenthorn, could not have been nicer and they happily looked after my stand until the final day when I went back north to dismantle it at the end of the Show. They are lovely people who run their own jewellery business in Nenthorn and I will always be grateful for the assistance they gave at a very difficult time.

In fact, the events surrounding my absence from home for some four days prompted a complete re-examination of what I was doing and Carol and I had a real heart-to-heart about the situation. Outwardly she had never been anything but full of encouragement for what I was trying to achieve, but, deep inside, she was unhappy - and justifiably so - because I had been spending so much time away from home, particularly at weekends attending fairs and shows. It didn't require a Brain of Britain to work out that her illness while I was at Aviemore was simply the culmination of some eighteen months of my to-ings and fro-ings, and I resolved that I would cut out a lot of the events which I had been doing. Many of them simply had not returned reasonable worth for the investment in the first place.

1992 finished on a high, with a very busy exhibition in my home town of Linlithgow yielding excellent sales, and a pre-Christmas craft fair at Ingliston (which Rainbow Fairs have regrettably decided not to arrange again) yielding further excellent income and orders. It proved a busy December.

PORT NIGH
The east coast of Kintyre offers splendid views to Arran - but four miles away - and the curve of the bay at Port Nigh, Carrodale, provides a lovely foreground.

AN INTRODUCTION TO COLD SELLING
(OR – AS ONE DOOR CLOSES ANOTHER ONE SHUTS)

If 1992 had closed with distinct signs of promise, my first venture into the world of cold selling in January 1993 almost had me turning tail within two hours and rushing home to dig a big hole!

With a great deal of expert advice from Carol, whose working life had basically been spent entirely in selling, I decided to use the winter months to build up outlets for the greeting cards. I set a daily target of six new outlets and, full of hope, with collar and tie and polished shoes, I headed first for Edinburgh.

It was a Tuesday morning. The Royal Mile in January is like Aberdeen on a flag day. At approximately half past ten, in my first call, I was told in no uncertain manner by a retailer of Scottish goods that he had no room for my stuff, it wasn't a line that he stocked (despite there being postcards in the shop!) and without saying so in so many words, obviously wondered why I was wasting his time. I left shattered.

Half an hour later, however, the lady owner of a shop just a little further up the Royal Mile gave me my first order of 50 cards but explained that she was not optimistic, especially since trade had been absolutely dreadful. A third call near the top of the Royal Mile produced a courteous 'no thank you' and so I headed for the glitz of Waverley Market, where the name of a young lady who ran one of the outlets there had been suggested to me as a possible customer.

She was nowhere to be seen when I arrived at the shop, but I wandered around for half and hour and did find her in on my return. She was very nice. She was also very sympathetic, and she seemed to like my samples. However, she hoped that I would understand that, having sold one pen throughout the course of the previous day, she was in no position to invest in new lines but thanked me for calling and wished me well.

At this point, I had made four calls to an area of the Capital City of Scotland which is normally (certainly in summer months) thronged with tourists looking for Scottish souvenirs and goods. In two hours, I had received one rude dismissal, one polite refusal, two tales of depressed trade and one order for fifty small greeting cards. You can possibly understand why my instinct was to head for home and disappear. However, faint heart never won fair maid and, suitably refreshed with the traditional lunchtime packet of crisps and Kit-Kat, I decided to brave the calls on the rest of my list during the afternoon. I was glad I did; I got two orders, one promise, one 'come back when the season starts' and no curt dismissals. It was therefore with some feeling of achievement that I returned home, virtually a nervous wreck, to report the days activity to my Sales Director!.

'But when he said that to you, why did you not say ….?!' said Carol. I looked at her blankly. 'And when the lady mentioned the poor trade, why did you not say ….?!' Carol asked again. Another blank stare. 'And when the bloke was rude to you, why didn't you say ….?!' A third blank expression.

For an hour, she went over tactics with me. It was like being back at school. The difference was that good and competent selling is a practised art over a number of years. Knowing exactly what to say in any given situation is an acquired skill. It was obvious that it was going to take a considerable amount of time before I could cope with the various comments which would be thrown at me by potential customers. Nevertheless, I carried on, and by the spring of 1993, I had some fifty outlets who were taking greeting cards and small mounted prints. I didn't think that was a bad start for an amateur.

With a much broader range of photographs covering much more of Scotland now, I am happy to report that greeting card sales, while hardly buoyant, are doing very nicely and the assistance of an enthusiastic Agent should hopefully see that position improve even more in the time ahead. Personally, I hope my days of cold calling are numbered; it is an extremely hard, and often thankless task.

In hindsight, I think that the closing months of 1992 and the early months of 1993 were unquestionably the turning point of the new business. The financial projections which I had done in the spring of 1991 had forecast that I would be in profit - albeit modest - by the end of the second year. Regrettably, the figures were still showing a loss but the regular deficiency of funds was being arrested - of that there was no doubt - and I was now genuinely optimistic that 1993 could at last put the business on a sound footing. If it turned out that way, it would be some one and a half years behind schedule (as Carol would continue to remind me!) but the combination of a severe recession and mistakes which I had made in trying to present the wrong product to my market had taken their toll; hopefully all would now be well.

BEN LOMOND
July, 4.30am-ish, just north of Duck Bay Marina on Loch Lomond - side. The sun has yet to make its appearance, but the pre-dawn light creates a great silhouette of the Ben and lovely reflections. Ten minutes later, there was no picture from this position

CUL MOR AND SUILVEN
Just one of a dozen pictures from Inverpolly and Assynt which might have been on this page. The fantastic sky, the width of the two mountains - and of course the tourist! - all made the trek up the hill behind Elphin well worth the effort.

INVERPOLLY AND ASSYNT

"When spring has melted its last corrie of snow, the amethyst escarpment of Ben More Coigach is a cloud city above the dark gateway to Loch Broom. The ochrous light of an autumn evening changes the jagged ridge of Stac Polly into the broken wall of a beleaguered Andalusian castle. In winter, all can be hidden by a frozen mist. When that is lifted, by sun or wind, mountain and moor are chalk-white and ink-black against a blue sky" - John Prebble.

It was a 2.30 am rise (With one of Carol's midnight horror movies on the bedroom T.V. until the early hours, was it really worth going to bed in the first place?!) I was in Ullapool for 6.30 am, only just beating a late October sunrise over the peaks of Inverlael and the five narrow miles or so of Loch Broom.

I had been in Inverpolly and Assynt once before - it was the summer of 1966 and the early days of the World Cup in England, by a strange coincidence. Only vague memories remained; sudden and dramatic mountains thrusting up from low, rocky, loch-spattered land; seemingly unending twists, turns, ups and downs of single track roadways with passing places. This photographic expedition I had therefore looked forward to with excitement and anticipation. It was a very long way to go (my round trip within the day would exceed four hundred miles) and I had to be as sure as possible that the light would be favourable, at least for the early part of the day. I was not disappointed.

The area is another of great fascination, both in its topography and in the derivations of its Gaelic or Norse place names. Loch Broom, for example, is derived from the Gaelic 'braon' meaning showers - how appropriate - although, to be fair, a great deal of the rain which is driven north-east on the prevailing winds exhausts itself over Applecross, Torridon and Flowerdale Forest before it reaches the Ullapool area.

Ullapool itself was founded in 1788 by the British Fisheries Society and it owes its existence to herring. Another of Scotland's endless photogenic townships, especially from the braes to the east of the village, it enjoys an idyllic situation on a thrusting peninsula into Loch Broom with, from the eastern slopes behind it, the flat top of Ben Ghoblach seemingly standing guard, despite its three mile distance from the village.

The herring boom lasted for about fifty years but it had vanished by 1880. The town has enjoyed (perhaps that is an unfortunate choice of word) varying fortunes in the fishing industry since then. This Autumn morning, it was sadly quiet.

I was too early for photographs of Ullapool; the sun needed at least an hour to climb over the shoulders of the mountains but after a reconnoitre to establish potential shots for later in the day, I hurried on northwards lest I should miss some spectacular morning light. (This is always one of the great frustrations of photography; if arrival at a location fails to coincide with the best light, the greatest composition in the world will never produce the stunning result that you are always looking for, and a combination of the two can be extremely difficult to obtain).

Such was the case as I rounded a bend and got my first glimpse of Loch Kanaird, with the southerly aspect of Ben More Coigach dropping down into the water. There is no peak to the mountain from this angle and again it was too early for the sun to light up the solid cliff wall. 'Coigach', by the way, is again Gaelic and literally means 'place of the fifths'; it derived from the ancient custom of dividing land into five parts.

One 'Coigach' later (work that out!) I was at Drumrunie Lodge and a tremendous picture opportunity presented itself within a lochan on the immediate left of the road reflecting autumnal trees, Stac Polly and Cul Beag; this shot unquestionably turned out to be one of the best of the day.

I had already decided to take the left turn on to the Achiltibuie road (the difficult decision was to come an hour or so later) and by this time the colour of the withering grass in the foreground, and on the slopes leading to the peaks of Ben More, was absolutely spectacular - it was almost orange. Again, a small lochan provided a mirror image of the steep northern slopes and from this angle, at last, a dramatic jagged peak of Ben More Coigach completed a lovely composition.

Stac Polly (only 2,009 ft) - which has been variously described as an aircraft carrier, like the palace of the Wizard of Oz, or a ruined Andalusian castle - was still regrettably in haze; the morning sun had not yet burned the low cloud off. The classic view of the mountain from the east end of Loch Lurgainn would have to await another visit, as would a climb to the top of one of the best viewpoints in Inverpolly. Stac Polly is a fairly easy climb (even for one with destroyed knees and advancing years!) and I look forward very much to the next visit - I won't miss the view from the top if the weather is kind.

Some ten minutes later it was decision time. I was nine miles or so along the road to Achiltibuie at the north west end of Loch Lurgainn. While the temptation was to continue west then round the corner to the village itself and the lovely views of the Summer Isles which are afforded from the rising ground behind it, I estimated that at least an hour and a half or perhaps two hours would be needed to do it justice. With so much of the spectacular scenery to the north of me and perhaps only two or three hours of good light ahead the coin had to be tossed again and the Summer Isles lost!

Before I turned right, however, I took a half mile walk or so along the western (and very boggy) shores of Loch Lurgainn to catch a lovely panorama looking back towards the rising sun; a wonderfully moody picture resulted which is still one of my favourites from the trip.

Back in the car, and now heading northwards on the single track road towards Lochinver, I had that sinking feeling again - had I done the right thing in turning my back on one of Scotland's renowned beauty spots and would I regret it? Within ten minutes, my fears were allayed as one view after another eastwards towards Inverpolly's mountainous monuments revealed new shapes and aspects to this lonely, rugged but beautiful place.

I pulled off the road, enjoyed a two or three hundred yard hike up a low hill, and got a wonderful shot of the morning sunlight on rocks, autumnal bracken and, in the distance, Suilven - 'The Sugar Loaf'.

Twenty minutes or so of further serpentlike twists and turns brought me to the seaweed-lined shore of Invekirkaig and then, in the village of Strathan, the branches and

fallen leaves of a rare deciduous tree formed a perfect framework for the little post office/general store and telephone box. It was to be my last shot for an hour and a half.

For a long time, I will not forget the feelings of disappointment which I experienced on entering Lochinver. I had a recollection from the mid sixties of twenty or thirty fishing boats in an extremely busy harbour, pretty westward facing cottages along the shoreline, and the end-on photographs of Suilven, from a location which I guessed to be northwest of the harbour, I knew to be spectacular. However, Lochinver's face had changed.

For a start the light had gone. A belt of cloud had killed the sunlight and how badly, at least that morning, Lochinver needed the sunlight. It is grey now, the harbour buildings are dull, purely functional, and debris was lying all around. The couple of fishing boats which were in harbour were rusting and sadly in need of attention. There was a complete absence of 'buzz' about the place - no nets, no lobster pots, no fishermen, no chatter - it was, frankly, morbid.

Eventually, I found the location for the shot of the houses with Suilven to the rear but unless I wanted a JCB, sewage pipes or other similar garbage in the frame, it was a non starter. With a feeling of dreadful disappointment - certainly the equal of that horrible day at Lower Largo - I left Lochinver behind and headed north.

The grey cloud which had been a problem for the past hour or so had begun to break up and I decided to take a left turn towards Stoer in the hope that I could come up with a reasonable shot or two. By the time I had reached the scattering of cottages which represents the village the skies had indeed cleared. An early afternoon sun was bathing the scene, and particularly the thousands upon thousands of round, smooth stones and boulders which lie packed together above the waterline on Stoer Bay.

It was a lovely experience. There was not a soul around. The beautiful colours of the water, the beach and the whitewashed cottages, and the continual thumping of the Atlantic as the waves broke on the beach created an audio-visual impact which no sound technician or cameraman could ever hope to transmit to an audience. Those were thirty magical minutes.

I missed out Achmelvich Bay simply because I was running out of time with so much yet to try and catch, came back to the main road and turned left. I caught the long southern aspect of Quinag from the southern leg of the boomerang that is Loch Assynt. The angle of the sun was all wrong some twenty minutes later to allow me to do justice to

DAYBREAK, INVERPOLLY
The half-mile slog through peat bogs to the western shore of Loch Lurgainn was well worth it
for this dramatic shot with a wide angle lens towards the early sun. The twenty eight mm
lens doesn't do the mountains justice, but there is still enough drama to make it a super shot.

Ardvreck Castle from the extreme eastern end of the loch, which was again a disappointment because I had read so much about it. (You can't do justice to Quinag either from this angle, catching only one of its seven sandstone peaks which rise to a high point of 2,653ft.)

The fame, or rather notoriety, of Ardvreck Castle was secured in the mid seventeenth century following the betrayal of the famed Marquis of Montrose, James Graham, by Neil MacLeod. It was a deed that MacLeod was to regret.

In 1650 Montrose had marched a depleted army south from Caithness to,once and for all, put down the Covenanters. He had anticipated help from the Clan Mackenzie but, in the mistaken belief that King Charles was trying a flanker with the Government of the time above Montrose's head, MacKenzie pulled out of the plans. At Invershin, Montrose's army was annihilated. He had his horse shot from underneath him but managed to escape to Assynt and landed at Ardvreck Castle.

There Neil MacLeod was ostensibly friendly towards him but betrayed him to his enemies. Montrose was promptly marched to the dungeons in Edinburgh and hanged in the Grassmarket. For his 'assistance', MacLeod was paid £20,000 and not a few tons of sour oatmeal. He immediately lost the respect of his neighbours, the Mackenzies, the clan chief of whom not unnaturally had a dreadful conscience for withdrawing his promised help to Montrose. In these days there were no Cabinet or Committee meetings; MacKenzie alone decided to devastate MacLeod's land and possessions, seized the whole of Assynt from the shamed traitor and subsequently Mackenzie and his clan enjoyed a hundred unbroken years as its masters.

Wonderful stuff - great history and yet sometimes, if the atmosphere is right, and you concentrate your gaze on former strategic strongholds like Ardvreck, Eilean Donan or Dunnottar, you can almost hear the clash of sword on shield, the popping of muskets or the screams of kilted Highland clansmen as they launch another attack; it's another wonderful bonus from the enjoyment of photography in the wild and lonely reaches of a land steeped in history.

I had romanticised enough for one day; it was afternoon now and the forecast band of cloud moving in from the Atlantic was not that far away. I wanted if possible to catch a view of Cul Mor and Suilven from the hillside above the little village of Elphin before I called it a day and I had to press on. I find when I am running out of light that

anxiety takes over. I worry that by passing up a promising photographic opportunity it will never be available again and, having hurried on to the next location, discover that it is perhaps not as dramatic as I had anticipated and then doubly regret the missed opportunity. Life's a bitch!

I got my shot of Suilven, now slightly hazy, some five miles to the west. An obliging sheep kindly turned away from me at exactly the right time to gaze at the panorama before us. I don't normally like people or animals in the frame but there are times when you need them for perspective or effect, and this was certainly one. She stood happily on the brow of a hill gazing westwards for a minute or two and the resulting photograph turned out to be one of the day's best.

(At this point, I would like to say to doubting members of my family or those customers who can't help thinking that some of the photographs we take are stage managed, that I do not carry stuffed sheep, cormorants, rabbits or other props in my camera bag for use as and when the need arises. Only real animals or birds may therefore apply for future modelling vacancies!)

My photographic day was nearly done; I had taken over a hundred pictures, about many of which I had great expectations. As normal I had a few disappointments along the way, the most notable of which were the dilemma over the Summer Isles and the sad state of Lochinver. Over the piece, however, the pluses far outweighed the minuses and a final half dozen shots of Ullapool being smiled upon by the last weakening rays of afternoon sun brought a long but very exciting day to a close.

I headed for Inverness, the A9 and home well satisfied. As usual I found that, far from being tired following a very early rise, a few miles of fairly strenuous walking over some difficult terrain, and the physical effort of humping sixty pounds of camera gear around the hills, I felt exhilarated. The anticipation and excitement of spending a day in and around what is arguably the most dramatic scenery in the United Kingdom had been more than justified. This time at least the route planning, poring over maps, research and study of articles and photographs of the area and, of course, the final gamble that the Meteorological Office had got it right for a change, had been well rewarded. Now - with the benefit of hindsight and the passage of time - it was just a fantastic trip.

AUTUMN ON THE TAY
An example of empty-handedness of previous visits paving the way for success on a future occasion. This magnificent beech tree, which threatens to fall into the river Tay, is bathed in wonderful autumn sunshine - and just look at the way in which the sun highlights the twists in the trunk.

"A lazy October sun began to light the hills above Faskally, slowly revealing a patchwork of greens, fawns and browns. Autumn frosts had already begun the destruction of Breadalbane's summer foliage. In sympathy with the steep slopes of Killiecrankie, the banks of the tumbling Garry, below, were yet in shadow.

Loch Tummel was still; the maiden's breast of Schiehallion awaited its escape from an early veil of mist. Later, Glen Lyon was rampant. When the sun had reached its high, the home of the Glencoe Campbells was awash with yellows, oranges and browns. Beyond Lawers, to the south, the boats had left Loch Tay, and the white-washed village of Kenmore was almost lost amidst the mass of autumnal splendour"
(Anon).

KENMORE
An extremely strenuous hike up Drummond Hill was worth every bead of sweat for this great
"aerial" picture of Kenmore and the technicolour which has photographers flocking to Perthshire
in autumn. The polarising filter darkens Loch Tay and accentuates further the riot of colour.

G oing back more years than I care to remember, I can yet recall the first quality photograph of the Scottish landscape which I ever took. My father had squeezed an afternoon off from his veterinary practice in Linlithgow, and suggested a run in the car through the Trossachs, past Lochearnhead and thence to Loch Tay - which I had never before seen. I suppose I would be around twelve.

I remember nothing at all about the trip apart from the photograph which I took of the Falls of Dochart with my Brownie 127; It was the classic tourist's picture, taken from the wall at the roadside to the west of the bridge over the river Dochart,, catching the falls themselves, and framing the Ben Lawers range in the distance with the fir trees on either side of the bridge. This was a black and white effort of course, but I can still see the 3" x 2" photograph as if it were yesterday.

It was this kind of outing, I am convinced, which began my love of the Scottish countryside; indeed it was the memory of that very trip which prompted me to return to the area shortly after I began my new career - in May, 1991 to be exact. I got some superb daybreak shots looking eastwards along Loch Tay, then in little Glen Quaich, Amulree and Aberfeldy.

Without a doubt, however, the time to see Perthshire is autumn. It is a veritable riot of colour in October, when approximately 200 square miles of the Perthshire landscape is every conceivable combination of yellows and greens, oranges and browns. Frankly, you have to see it to believe it.

Several customers had asked for autumn shots of Glen Lyon, the Hermitage and the Falls of Braan at Dunkeld, and, of course, the Queen's View of Loch Tummel. To date, I had nothing to satisfy them. I had nothing of Pitlochry and a fairly ordinary shot of Kenmore. Even Schiehallion had remained elusive as far as a quality photograph was concerned.

Breadalbane is Campbell country, believe it or not, and the Campbells who were responsible for the slaughter of the MacDonalds in Glencoe in 1692, hailed from Glen Lyon.

Perthshire, in fact, is steeped in ancient history and was the furthest point north which the Romans reached almost 2000 years ago. If you listen long and hard enough to the residents of the village of Fortingall, they will convince you that Pontius Pilate was born there! (Thanks to the bar-man in the local hotel, through the passage of time this story becomes more and more like the fisherman's tale and gains in credulity each time he tells it. It's a pity that Pontius Pilate was born years before the Romans entered Britain for the first time!).

There is a wealth of history across the whole of Perthshire. I will confine my recall of such to the period between 1774 and 1780 when, on Schiehallion, experiments were begun in an attempt to judge the weight of the earth. A cairn commemorating the efforts of the Astronomer Royal and of Charles Hutton (who invented contour lines as a result of their work) now marks the event in the car park from which you ideally begin the ascent of "The Maiden's Breast". It is one of the finest walks in Scotland. The mountain was, many years ago, a place of worship for the Picts in the time before Christianity reached Scotland and its name directly derives from that - "The Fairy Mountain of the Caledonians".

The Perthshire countryside is as beautiful as its history is bloody, particularly in October, and my plans for this autumn visit centred on an early morning start atop Craigower, a hill to the immediate north of Pitlochry. Once again, Bartholemew's handbook came into its own and I hoped to arrive in good time for sunrise and enjoy the wonderful views down the Garry and west towards Rannoch. The necessity to begin the ascent through Pitlochry Golf Course would allow the bonus of a few shots on the way down although I would probably have done the Club more justice had I been able to come back in the afternoon when the light would have been from a more favourable angle.

It was 6am on a cold October morning when I reached Pitlochry, beating the sunrise, and causing a change of plan. Having a quick look at Loch Faskally, whose waters were a sheet of glass, I envisaged the wonderful reflection of a red morning sky on the water and therefore stood shivering on the banks of the loch for three quarters of an hour as disappointing whites, creams and pale yellows accompanied an unspectacular dawn.

So I headed back to Pitlochry and, indeed, the walk to the top of Craigower. Laden with camera gear, it's a fairly stiff climb but well worth the effort as the views from the top encompass the little village of Moulin and the southward passage of the river Garry, the hillsides opposite above Faskally, the long valley of Strathtummel, which Queen Victoria came to love so much, past Schiehallion to Rannoch and ultimately Glencoe.

The rising sun gradually lit the tree-covered hillsides above Loch Faskally then the north shores of Loch Tummel and I got three or four super shots of this great stretching panorama to the west.

As usual, however, anxieties about just how long this lovely light would last

AUTUMN IN GLEN LYON
I spent ages in this little copse beside the river before I was happy with the composition -
there was so much that might have been included. It doesn't do justice to this loveliest of
Perthshire Glens in autumn, but it's still a cracking picture!

caused less time to be spent on the hill than I might have wished. After a twenty or thirty minute stop around the closing holes of the golf club, I was back in the car, heading for Killiecrankie and the left turn towards Loch Tummel.

The traditional "Queen's View" picture was cracking in the early morning light. It wasn't easy to exclude the caravans or a few stray tourists (even this early in the morning!) but, well satisfied, I headed along the shores of the Loch and was then rewarded with the most glorious autumn birch tree framing Shiehallion. There was nothing terribly spectacular in either Strathtummel or Tummel Bridge, where I turned left into Keltney Burn Glen, and at Coshieville I took the the right turn towards Fortingall and thence Glen Lyon.

The glen is some twenty five miles in length, with scattered remains of keeps and castles to be seen. It is the twelve miles or so of the eastern end which is so dramatic; steep sides to the valley - both to the south and to the north. The sheer height of the southern slopes (which in fact are the northern side of the Lawers range) created a wall which the October sun could not overcome to fully light the wonderful colours in the bottom of the valley far below, where the river Lyon tumbled and gurgled its way towards Loch Tay.

Happily, however, the sun created some spectacular colour schemes higher up the hillsides but the difficult lighting made it impossible to do justice to the whole valley. I ended up with an amazing shot of a " moss floor' - a vivid green carpet creeping around some lovely beech trees. While the much sought-after panorama of the whole glen remained elusive, I was more than happy with that localised composition - it has been an excellent seller.

I drove slowly up the glen marvelling at the colours, and only regretting that, on this trip at least, I wasn't able to do more justice to the overall scene. I drove as far as the Bridge of Balgie, where I had hoped to carry on to the far end of the glen - it flattens out but is no less spectacular for that as it becomes "Rannochlike" in its remoteness, but repairs had closed the road. The minor road south over Ben Lawers was also closed off and I therefore had to retrace my steps. That was a disappointment but there was a bonus of a shot of Ben Lawers with some autumn snow on it and some lovely angry clouds behind. The fact that the photograph was taken from the northern, rather than the southern side, made it just that bit different.

It was now the middle of the afternoon and, having had a further brief look at Fortingall I turned right and headed into Fearnan on the banks of Loch Tay, and the few

further miles eastward to Kenmore where I had planned the last outing of the day.

The ascent of Drummond Hill, behind Kenmore, can be attempted from either of two car parks; I opted for the one to the north of the new holiday development where an excellent nine hole golf course is proving to be an enjoyable test for keen holiday golfers. The climb to Black Crag, which has a wonderful grandstand view of the eastern end of Loch Tay and the village of Kenmore, was a hard one but the paths are good and the mile and a half or so of zig-zags is well worth the effort for the spectacular result - given good light, of course.

I was lucky in that the late afternoon weather was clearing. Some tremendous sunshine was lighting up the whitewashed houses and the church in the village as I reached my target. Already there, and enjoying the view, were two young Australian students, one of whom was fighting with a compact camera in an attempt to capture some classic Scottish countryside for subsequent despatch to his homeland. I hope my advice helped - for their part, I think they enjoyed the look of Kenmore through my zoom lens as I gave them the opportunity to see what an SLR camera fitted with a polariser could do!

I was nearly satisfied for the day; the walk down to the car park was an awful lot easier than the walk up and, with the sun now steadily sinking below the hills to the west of Loch Tay, I had but a few minutes left to capture a late afternoon shot against the sun using a lonely tree on the very edge of the water to frame a nice view of Ben Lawers.

There was patently to be no spectacular sunset so I headed east to Aberfeldy and turned right towards Amulree to enjoy an evening drive through the Sma' Glen. I stopped briefly at the ascent out of Aberfeldy to enjoy the lovely view northwards towards Drummond Hill, Schiehallion in the distance and Ben Lawers to the north west and felt well satisfied with yet another spectacular day.

Nothing I had previously read, nor have seen or studied since, has been overstated about this most glorious of sights. Perthshire in autumn is a "must" for anyone who particularly loves the splendours of our technicolour autumn; with the possible exception of Glen Affric in Invernesshire, the hills and glens of Perthshire are unrivalled.

MEALL GORM
A classic Scottish landscape to which the camera cannot properly do justice; the cliff face of
Meall Gorm, from high up on the Bealach na Ba -arguably Scotland's most astonishing "feet"
of roadway engineering, up and over the Applecross peninsula.

Torridon contains some of the world's most ancient substructure of rock. Geologists tell us that Lewisian Gneiss ranks alongside the oldest in the world (around 3000 million years) and the Torridon sandstones were laid upon this ancient base around one and a half billion years ago. Erosion then began to create the drama of the landscape we are now lucky enough to witness across Torridon, Inverpolly and Assynt. If you haven't been there and marvelled at it, you have missed one of the great wonders of the Scottish landscape.

My first trip to Inverpolly and Assynt, as you will observe from the chapter covering that most memorable of photographic days, required a major decision to be taken at roughly 6.30am in the morning some 170 miles from home, on the road to Achiltibuie.

On this occasion, when I reached the village of Garve, some twenty five miles north west of Inverness, there was no hesitation. My destination was Torridon, but as I was to discover - yet again, unexpectedly - the real bonus of the trip came in Applecross and around Loch Carron.

I had company on this trip; Carol's cousins from Norwich were enjoying two weeks' holiday in Scotland (I always look forward to them coming because they never fail to bring good weather with them!) and Terry, who was brought up in Wick, loves exploring the country. I knew he would appreciate a visit to a part of Scotland which he had never seen.

Our original plan was to leave around 4am, head for the golf courses around the Cromarty and Dornoch Firths and then, mid-morning, after a visit to the course at Strathpeffer, we would head west to Kinlochewe and the surprises of the Torridon area. Not for the first time, the weather dictated otherwise.

Forecasts for the third week in August were, frankly, horrible. Looking ahead from the weekend, all the forecasters were predicting wind, heavy showers and prolonged rain in the north west, although indications also were that, later each day, the rain would ease and some sunny periods develop. Terry was delighted to hear, therefore, that I was postponing the 4am departure and, instead, I picked him up at his holiday chalet in Linlithgow around 7am.

Apart from some annoyance with three heavily-laden articulated lorries on the A9 (a speed of 35 m.p.h. or thereby on the stretch from Kingussie to Carrbridge being made even more irritable by the second and third vehicles cramming the one in front - why are some H.G.V. drivers so selfish?) the journey to Inverness was uneventful. Contrary to forecasts, the weather looked highly promising and there was some superb early morning sun lighting up the Tummel Valley as we turned north-west out of Killiecrankie. It was thus a disappointment to find, on reaching the descent into Inverness, that clouds had thickened, rain started to fall, and as we crossed the Kessock Bridge, there was every sign that the weather further north was indeed forbidding. I reluctantly abandoned the idea of visits to Dornoch and Tain; with Strathpeffer under heavy cloud, it wasn't difficult to decide to keep going.

In fact the weather deteriorated for the next hour and the cross-country stage of the journey was punctuated by showers and ever-lowering cloud. That 'I hate weather forecasters' syndrome was beginning to assert itself again and I was feeling doubly annoyed because Terry, especially, had been looking forward so much to his first view of the Western Highlands.

We made our first stop at the lay-by at Loch Achanalt, where despite the gloom, I took a couple of shots across the water, of crofters' cottages and some low wispy cloud blowing across the tops of the hills. The light was, frankly, awful, but despair does funny things to a photographer and somehow I thought this might turn out to be shot of the day!

There was some encouragement ahead, however, as we turned into the long descent through Glen Docherty towards the west end of Loch Maree, and noticed that Kinlochewe, some five miles further on, was enjoying blinks of sunshine. In the right light, this end-on shot of Loch Maree (which I haven't yet seen anywhere) would be an absolute cracker, but it requires either the valley to be flooded by early morning sun, or a really dramatic Spring or Autumn sunset to make the shot.

True, the clouds had thinned a little as we reached Kinlochewe (apparently, for those intending a visit to this busy little 'junction', the local exchange rate is two bottles of whisky to a salmon!). I opted for 'plan A' rather than 'plan B'; plan A was to turn left at Kinlochewe, park at Loch Clair, some three miles down the road, and enjoy a mile or so of the walk along the north shore, hopefully to capture the views of Beinn Eighe and Liathach, which are both so dramatically prominent from that most productive of walks in Torridon. (The rest of plan A, by the way, involved retracing our steps to Kinlochewe, following the road along the south of Loch Maree, up to Gairloch, and, if time permitted, a visit to Poolewe and Inverewe Gardens, thence back to Kinlochewe, south to Torridon, Sheildaig and, ultimately, the Applecross peninsula).

Despite the absence of good light, it was a lovely calm morning. While it was just late enough to catch the mirrored reflections of the mountains on Loch Clair (so vividly described in that tremendous 'Companion Guide' to the west coast of Scotland by W H Murray "The West Highlands of Scotland") there was, at least, some promise in the sky. It now threatened to break a little and, on our way back from the east end of Loch Clair, offered a few shots of the cloud-topped ridges of both mountains. Failure to see their quartzite tops, from this angle, however, was a major disappointment and photographic justice to both must await another day.

The ridge and peaks of Beinn Eighe (pronounced 'A' as in 'air') provide some of the classic mountain walks of Scotland. Those who venture up are rewarded with sight of rare wild life (ptarmigans, wild cats, pine martens, golden eagles) and, ultimately, fabulous views northwards; from Slioch - closest to you - across some really savage peaks to An Teallach, south of Loch Broom. There are seven tops across the seven mile ridge of 'The File' (the meaning of 'Eighe') and while the greater density of the mountain is of red sandstone, the Cambrian Quartzite of it's four eastern summits gives, in the right light,, a shining white glow to this most dramatic of mountains. The climbs are not for the faint-

hearted (and certainly not for an ageing photographer with football injuries!) and you must be well planned, clothed and carry ample provisions in case of trouble.

If, like me, you can't or won't attempt an ascent of either Beinn Eighe or Liathach, content yourself with the walk from Loch Clair, past Loch Coulin, through the Coulin Forest (not of trees, but of deer) along the valley of the river of the same name to Achnashellach, in Glen Carron; the best 10 miles in Wester Ross, according to the experts.

So we made our way back to Kinlochewe, turned left and headed up the shores of Loch Maree. Perhaps in the top three or four of Scotland's most beautiful inland lochs, (Loch Lomond and Loch Awe are certainly close rivals) Loch Maree is dominated - from whichever angle you view it - by the 3,217 feet of magnificent Slioch, and made prettier by the wealth of trees which, in this part of Scotland anyway, are a sight for sore eyes. The north western half of Loch Maree's twelve mile stretch is, like the southern half of Loch Lomond, spattered by islands, many wooded, and the most unlikely of broad-leaved trees still flourish.

Again, the light was depressingly grey with only an occasional ray or two of sun, and the conning-tower of Slioch was, like it's neighbours a few miles to the south, swathed in cloud. I took a few shots but, to be honest, if you can't see the top five hundred feet of Slioch, you could be shooting the picture anywhere in Scotland, call it 'Loch Maree and Slioch' and nobody would know any better - the third (or was it fourth?) disappointment of the day.

It was now late morning. As we drove through the valley of the river Kerry and looked disdainfully at the destruction of thousands of trees on what was, formerly, a very attractive approach to Gairloch, the greyness of the day, if anything, got worse.

The pretty little harbour at An Ard, half a mile east of Gairloch, offered the opportunity for a couple of shots, as a bright patch of sky to the south contrasted starkly with the general grey all around, and created some nice reflections on the surface of the water in the harbour. Regrettably, the brightness did not reach the village of Gairloch itself a few minutes later. Another disappointment from the trip was marked up as I attempted to make something of , first, the scattered houses in this prettiest of West Highland villages, second, the fantastic lichen on the rocks to the west of the beach, and, lastly, of the sandy bay itself. But what a glorious winter picture this would make - low sun on the water, the sandy beach, and, most dramatic of all, lighting up the little church which overlooks the whole panorama.

SUNSET, LOCHCARRON:
At the end of a long and often frustrating day, this superb panorama looking to Skye was presented to us with clearing skies and lovely evening light.

There was a bonus, however, as I managed a nice shot of the little nine hole golf course behind the beach. The lofty tops of Baosbheinn and Beinn An Eoin in the background create a dramatic backdrop to the views of the course from the promontory at the south-east of the village. I hoped it would ultimately make the pages of the 1995 'Home of Golf' handbook on which I was currently working.

There were signs of another bonus, however, as the break in the sky which we had seen to the south took on a highly promising appearance over the next half hour. For the third time that day, we drove into Kinlochewe and turned south towards Torridon.

Regrettably, the skies had not broken enough to allow the sunshine to illuminate the little houses of Torridon village, completely overwhelmed by the mass of Liathach which rears so suddenly, seemingly from the back gardens. The mountain's own magnificent features were, sadly, either invisible because of the low cloud on the summit, or completely lost in the flatness of the grey light. At this point in the trip, I had my greatest sense of non-fulfilment as I had thought that this particular view of Torridon and Liathach would be one of the major highlights and make a superb picture. One day I'll learn not to count chickens . . . .

The rising ground to the south of Loch Torridon not only provides excellent views of Liathach but also of Beinn Alligin - given the right circumstances these would make stunning shots - but the promised break in the weather looked as if it was about to materialise as we arrived in Sheildaig and decided to have a bite to eat. A pretty little village this, again with great photographic potential in the right light; I bagged a couple of 'record' shots and we headed off towards Kishorn with the distinct promise of some nice late afternoon weather at last.

Some twenty five minutes later, we were turning right at Tornapress to begin the ascent over the Bealach na Ba ("The Pass of the Cattle") where reputation has it that the most popular spot on the 12-mile road over to Applecross is a passing place - I understand why, now! I had heard about it, I had read about it, but I had never seen it. My expectations were more than fulfilled, not only by the scarcely credible construction of a road which passes, literally, across the very top of a mountain, but just as excitingly, by the long awaited appearance of some decent sunshine.

As we slowly climbed (second gear at best) the twisting single track road to reach around 2,500 feet, the views back down the pass were breathtaking. The little houses at Achiltraid, on the shore of Loch Kishorn (you can't actually see Kishorn itself because of the bluffs of Bheinn Bhan - 'the-white Mountain') are even tinier than those which in Torridon village cower at the foot of Liathach. They provided a great composition with the vertical cliffs of Meall Gorm. Some lovely light at last began to provide the right conditions for decent photography.

Another steep half mile, still in second gear, brought us to the plateau at the top of Meall Gorm, and to the little car park: A two minute stroll opened up what must be one of the most spectacular landscapes in Scotland. With visibility now first class, the mountains of the Glenelg Peninsula and Knoydart stood out to the south east; then came the Ardnamurchan Peninsula, the dramatic jaggedness of Rhum, then the Red Hills behind Broadford, the Cuillins, Dun Caan's table-top on Raasay and finally the hills of Trotternish on Skye's north-west peninsula. The lowering evening sun was still strong and it didn't make for straightforward photography; a grey graduated filter, however, came into it's own and I was optimistic at the prospects of the shots doing the scene justice. Unexpectedly, and suddenly, the trip was beginning to pay dividends.

The descent into Applecross is almost an anti-climax - it could hardly be anything else - but this delightful little village, together with it's neighbour Milltown threw up lots more possibilities before we turned around and headed back towards the Bealach na Ba.

As we crossed Meall Gorm on our return journey, we marvelled again at the audacity of those brave souls who, hundreds of years ago, had decided to drive their cattle from a landing point at Applecross over terrain which, in those days, must have been almost impassable. I hope we never get to the stage where we take all those pioneering feats of engineering for granted. On this evening in Applecross we added another to the list.

Incidentally, a word of caution; the local Highways Department have made it quite clear, with warning notices at each end of the road, that it is liable to be impassable during all of the winter months. I estimate that, from sea level to the plateau of Meall Gorm there must have been a drop in temperature of at least 10° so if you plan to make the trip be well clothed, even in summer.

We had now been on the road for around twelve hours; while it would be unfair to say that the first eleven had been wasted from a photographic point of view, it is one of the great frustrations of the profession that you have to go so far, and sometimes wait so long for an opportunity.

Having come back down to earth, as it were, the four mile trip across the pass between Kishorn and Loch Carron did not take long. It took even less time to find The Bothy in Lochcarron where dinner was quickly ordered! The Loch was absolutely still, the evening sun had created some great light, and while I waited for a bowl of home made soup to arrive, I nipped out and took a few shots along the water side. Having now finished off the third roll of film for the day, I packed away camera bodies, lenses, tripods etc., as I was fairly sure my work was done for the day. I was mistaken.

Suitably fed and watered, the first thing I did was telephone home to advise Carol that an expected return time of around 10pm was now delayed by approximately 2 hours! Naturally, I blamed Terry for faffing around with his video; in truth I had underestimated the amount of time we would spend crossing the Bealach na Ba (and getting back again) and the two or three chunks of twenty minutes or so we spent hanging around awaiting better light had simply compounded the lateness. It was proving a long day.

A quick look at the golf course at Loch Carron on the way past allowed me to make some mental notes for the golf handbook and, ten minutes later, we were climbing the south side of Loch Carron towards Strome Ferry. The light was simply fantastic.

We had left Lochcarron at precisely 8pm, The Bothy having done an excellent job with home-made lentil soup and an enormous helping of deep fried haddock. The clearance of cloud from the sky had continued as we drove down the south-eastern side of the loch and completed the ascent which, just a few miles from Plockton, affords magnificent views south-west towards the mouth of the loch, Kishorn and Skye. The road was deserted so there was plenty of time to admire the late evening moods of a truly beautiful corner of the western Highlands.

Near the top of the hill we pulled on to a grassy verge - it hadn't started its life as that but numerous visitations during the summer by traffic like ours had created a convenient viewpoint, destroying another chunk of Scotland's natural vegetation in the process, of course.

Terry already had at least half a minute on video tape (hopefully with commentary which would do justice to the beauty and tranquillity of the scene) before I found the spot

I was looking for to take some shots of my own. So engrossed were we both in our respective attempts to commit a Lochcarron sunset to film that we were completely unaware of another vehicle joining us.

It was only when I heard the unmistakable tones of a female Australian voice that I turned to find a highly excited couple in full Highland dress, the lady belting away with her compact and the gentleman putting another hurried 30 seconds or so of a Scottish sunset on tape. Within a few weeks, I imagined it would be boring the pants off neighbours and relatives down under! He was back behind the wheel in less than a minute.

The lady broke the silence. 'You look as if you are taking serious photographs' she opined. I explained that it was now my living. She turned to the car and shouted for her husband. Somewhat reluctantly, I thought, he came out to greet me. The lady explained to him that I was a professional landscape photographer and, without another word, he was back in the car and returned seconds later, with a compliments slip carrying the name of his business in Australia. 'The only Scottish shop in Sydney' he said 'send me some of your stuff and I'll have a look at it'. Who needs foreign trade exhibitions when new export business like this is around?!

I asked the lady how long they were staying in Scotland. 'Actually it's half-holiday, half-business', she said. 'We're on our way down south to see my friend before we head home. She stays in Norwich'.

Terry, having completed his latest Attenborough-like epic, was already back in my car. 'Where in Norwich does your friend live?' I asked. 'A little place called Dereham' replied the Australian lady. I couldn't contain my surprise and explained that Terry's mother-in-law had lived in Dereham until very recently. Excitedly, she rushed round to the passenger side of the car and thus, a further twenty five minutes or so behind schedule, we eventually bade our goodbyes and headed south again. It is a small world.

Photographically, that concluded my attempts for the day to put this small world on cellulose. As usual in the Western Highlands, good light remained in the sky until almost Fort William, although it just wasn't light enough, paradoxically, to allow us the enjoyment of the drama of Glencoe an hour or so before midnight.

Nineteen hours after I had left West Calder, we arrived home and managed not to waken the household by rattling keys, tripping over the dog or falling upstairs. Despite sleeping on and off for the last three hours of the journey, Terry was absolutely exhausted (the next morning he couldn't even remember climbing into his bed) but, as usual, my head was still too full of everything we had seen that day to allow tiredness to overcome me. It had been another wonderful trip - 553 miles in total - and now, only one regret remains from the day's adventures.

The Torridon photographs, as I had suspected, turned out 'flat'. Despite the planning, the reading and the continual examination of weather forecasts, pictures to do justice to this legendary part of Scotland remain elusive to me. The late Applecross and Lochcarron shots, however, undid a lot of the earlier frustrations, and aside from professional pursuits, it had been yet another memorable day which, as ever, had yielded plenty of surprises.

TWEEDDALE
A favourite view of the Tweed from the high ground to the west of Manor Bridge, near
Peebles, with the vibrant colours of early spring cradling this popular stretch of the river.

At the time of writing, almost four years into my new career, I have perhaps around twelve hundred pictures in my portfolio of the Scottish landscape.

There are hundreds - nay, thousands - of places and locations I have yet to visit. Some of these are ridiculously close at hand and often I wonder about the logic of their not appearing on the list while lots of other far-flung locations, or some which are very difficult to reach, have been given preferential treatment.

Having read so many books about Scotland now, and having looked at so many pictures taken by a variety of our top Scottish photographers, a yearning to see them all for myself builds up and they are soon on the board in my office under 'shots required'.

In stark contrast, there are locations which feature over and over again in my portfolio. My home town of Linlithgow is an obvious example, as I now have around forty pictures of the town and the surrounding area. Others which feature strongly, and which I have visited regularly, include the East Neuk of Fife, the East Lothian coastline, the Peebles area and the Trossachs.

On the other hand, despite visiting some areas of Scotland on several occasions, I have yet to capture a quality photograph for inclusion in the portfolio. Twice, for example, I have made the trip to the Plockton area but feel that I have not done this most beautiful of West Highland villages justice with the camera. The first time it was because of poor weather, the second, the wrong time of day to catch the sunlight on the village. For the same reasons - and despite being in the vicinity on perhaps eight or ten occasions - I still have no quality pictures of Ben Nevis. Four times I have been to Kintail, but still don't have the stunning shot of the Five Sisters which I dearly want; and if, by the time this book is published, I don't have a picture of Ben Ledi taken from the high ground to the east of Callander, I promise that 'wanted' posters of Ian McAskill will be plastered all over the town!

Having said all that, I have been very lucky on other occasions when a first visit to a location about which I knew very little except what I had read or inspected of other

SUNRISE AT THE BASS ROCK
Again, a lot of pre-planning, a very early start (3.30am) and, regrettably, an undramatic sunrise behind the hulk of Bass Rock. Nevertheless a much-admired picture.

peoples' work, yielded another addition to the portfolio. I think particularly of an early morning burst of sun over St. Mary's Loch; a tremendous shot of old Stirling Brig' with the Wallace Monument in 'ghost mode' under a storm-cloud in the background; I think of my favourite golf course shot (still) showing the flag at the Road Hole at St. Andrews with the R and A clubhouse in the background; I think of the wonderful autumn colours in Kelvingrove when I made my first photographic trip to Glasgow. I could go on and on with the tales of disappointments and surprises but I think you get the message!

From all my scourings and scavenging of the Scottish countryside, I have listed some of my favourite locations in the hope that you may, on a visit of your own sometime in the future, capture the atmosphere and beauty of the place. Hopefully, light and weather permitting, you will succeed in your own attempt to do justice to the scene with your camera.

SUMMER REFLECTIONS, LINLITHGOW
The classic view of Linlithgow Loch, Palace and St. Michael's Church which must have been painted and photographed as often as any other historical building in Scotland. Lovely August morning sunshine highlights the eastern wall of the Palace, and of course, Sir Basil Spence's controversial "Crown of Thorns" on the kirk.

LOTHIAN REGION

LINLITHGOW

The views across the loch to the Palace and St. Michael's Church. Despite my bias, this has to be one of the most beautiful of all settings for ancient historical buildings across the whole of Scotland. A different mood in every season.

BATHGATE HILLS

The views, first, from the Knock eastwards to the Bridges, the Forth Estuary, Edinburgh and the Pentlands and, second, westwards from Cairnpapple towards the Fintry Hills, Stirling, the Trossachs and the Ochil Hills are stunning on a clear day.

EDINBURGH

the classic view of the City from Arthur's Seat is still one of the greatest in Scotland; the 180° turn which then reveals the whole of East Lothian and the Lammermuir Hills is only spoiled by the power station at Cockenzie.

NORTH BERWICK

the view from Berwick Law-all 360° of it!; the dramatic view of the gannet-strewn Bass Rock from Canty Bay on the Tantallon Road; Tantallon Castle, from the fields on the little road down to Seacliff.

TYNINGHAME SANDS

one of the loveliest spots on the whole of the East coast; dunes, rocks, the sea and a lovely northward aspect of Bass Rock.

MORNING SUNLIGHT, ST. MARY'S LOCH;-
Conveying perfectly the atmosphere of James Hogg's stamping ground, this lovely moody
shot owes its existence to a timely burst of early morning sun through some pretty dark
cloud and a grey graduated filter. Still one of my favourite pictures.

GOAT FELL
Taken from the ferry approaching the island; a fairly fast speed (with fingers crossed that I had the horizon level); I waited until I had the mountain and castle in opposite corners of the frame before shooting. To me, this picture says "ARRAN"!

DUNOON PIER
Late afternoon sunshine on this striking Dunoon landmark proved irresistible.
I used the ageing timbers in the foreground because I thought
they were totally consistent with the mood.

LAMLASH AND HOLY ISLAND
There are few trees on the golf course at Lamlash but these ones, behind the first green,
with the sun casting dramatic shadows towards me, perfectly framed the flag,
the town and Holy Island.

CHAPTER VII

THE BORDERS

ST. ABBS HEAD

one of the finest coastal/cliff top walks in Scotland with wonderful picture taking
opportunities all around - sunrise from the cliff-tops is fabulous.

SCOTT'S VIEW

on the B6356 between Earlston and Dryburgh; it has all been said before
- a stunning view in all seasons but try to catch it in autumn light.

ST. MARY'S LOCH

gorgeous in the early morning with the hills all around reflected on one of the
most tranquil surfaces of water in Scotland.

TWEEDDALE

photographic locations everywhere but my favourite is looking down on Manor
Bridge, just west of Peebles.

FLOORS CASTLE, KELSO

arguably the Borders' most beautiful stately home; a lovely autumnal scene from
the high ground south of the Tweed.

LAUDER COMMON

the high spot on the road from Lauder over to Stow; glorious rolling hills with
gorgeous browns in late winter after ploughing.

MOFFAT WATER

The Grey Mare's Tail takes all the glory in the valley of the Moffat Water but the
view south down the valley itself is just superb.

MONREITH BAY
Looking north from a vantage point above St. Medans on the west coast of the
Mull of Galloway; a simple shot with the height emphasising the sweep of the bay.

DUMFRIES & GALLOWAY

DALVEEN PASS

a lovely and much under-rated half mile or so beneath the southern slope of Lowther Hill on the A702 between the A74 and Thornhill.

DAYBREAK ON THE SOLWAY

Southerness, to be exact, but anywhere along the estuary of the Nith or the Solway Firth will prove to be an excellent location.

KIPPFORD

for afternoon or evening when the sun will catch the houses; a dirty, muddy estuary when the tide is out but very photogenic with abundant picture-taking possibilities.

MONREITH BAY

on the west coast of the Mull of Galloway, south of Port William; the view northwards from the cliff tops, just before St. Medans golf course, is wonderful - again late afternoon or evening.

FIFE

EAST NEUK

superb compositions everywhere, through Elie, St. Monans, Anstruther, Pittenweem, Cellardyke and Crail. For something different, take yourself to the cliffs above Kincraig Bay (west of Elie) and try a late afternoon or evening shot back towards Elie, Earlsferry and Isle of May - stunning. The other East Neuk towns must have some kind of world record for being photographed so try making your own composition using the nets, floats, boat colours and houses along the harbours. If you don't come away from here with some really cracking photographs, sell the camera!

DYSART

virtually unknown (outside of Fife!); fishing harbour and National Trust restored sea-front cottages make this an unexpected but beautiful bonus to any Fife trip.

WEST WEMYSS

As Dysart (above) - beautifully restored.

LOMOND HILLS

little photographed but with great potential, especially from the unclassified road which goes north from the village of Leslie towards Falkland.

ST ANDREWS

lovely, if undramatic, views of the old cathedral from the east side of the harbour using the boats and the estuary of the burn to frame it; superb view of east beach and the town from the foot of the caravan park at Kinkell.

SUNSET, LOCH LOMOND
A very hard climb up Conic Hill, a two hour wait but a rewarding picture; again, regrettably, it fails to convey the breadth of the panoramas from this vantage point above Balmaha.

STRATHCLYDE (NORTH OF THE RIVER)

LOCH LOMOND

the classic view looking north from Duncryne Hill (near Gartocharn) with all the islands before you and wonderful views of the Arrochar Alps and Balmaha then Ben Lomond to your right (early afternoon, ideally). From the top of Conic Hill (behind Balmaha). A very stiff climb but worth it to stand atop the Highland Boundary Fault itself with the islands of the loch strung out below you south-westerly. One of the best sunset positions in Scotland if you're lucky.

INVERARAY

classic view of the town, the Castle and Loch Fyne from the Bell Tower to the north of the village; a stiff walk but worth every bead of sweat.

LOCH AWE

glorious views from all banks; the best known is the southern aspect of Kilchurn Castle, with mountainous Hinterland all around (try to hide the power lines and pylons!).

LOCH ETIVE

the eastward view from North Connel, or from Dunstaffnage Castle at Dunbeg, is classic Scotland with Ben Cruachan overlooking Etive's easternmost shores.

LOCH ARKLET

again on the single track road from Aberfoyle to Inversnaid, one occasion when you can 'leap out of the car' and fire away! You look westwards to Ben Ime and Ben Vane - a classic panorama.

STRATHCLYDE (SOUTH OF THE RIVER)

AILSA CRAIG

'Paddy's Milestone' dominates views from the Ayrshire coast from, roughly, Ayr southwards. I have three favourites; the first from the coastal road just south of Dunure with Culzean Castle in the left-middle distance. The second is from the tenth tee of the Ailsa course at Turnberry and includes the lighthouse - a wonderful composition and one which took me three visits to capture! The third is a dramatic view from the road south of Ballantrae as it heads up the hill from the village. Looking back down over the town to Ailsa Craig (using a telephoto lens) will give me a great shot one day.

ARRAN

sunset behind Arran from anywhere on the north Ayrshire coast is one of the classic sights of Scotland; try it from the vicinity of Prestwick St. Nicholas golf course. The 'Sleeping Warrior' is also visible from many other parts of the mainland, including Conic Hill above Balmaha on Loch Lomond - some twenty five miles distant. As for the island itself, the view of Brodick Bay and Goat Fell as the ferry approaches the island is splendid; the rising ground to the south of Brodick gives a lovely view of the bay and Goat Fell again and the mountain ridge is beautiful when viewed from the road which splits Arran in half between Blackwaterfoot and Brodick. Try the view of Pladda and Ailsa Craig from the very southward tip of the island - a great combination. Lastly, the island from Kintyre (but four miles away) is magnificent.

COWAL PENINSULA

Glendaruel - wonderful autumn colours - best viewed from the little road to Otter Ferry.

KYLES OF BUTE

from Kyles of Bute G.C. above Tighnabruaich (around the ninth tee!).

LOCH ARKLET
A perfect example of how bad weather never prevents atmospheric picture taking; a foul rain shower but tremendously powerful clouds above the western extremity of the Trossachs.

STORMY AFTERNOON, SOUTH MORAR
An afternoon of heavy showers and bursts of sun were the catalysts for this
shot from the white sands of Morar looking to Eigg and Rhum.
The dramatic skyscape steals the show, however.

EILEAN DONAN CASTLE
Storm clouds, bursts of sun and the finest vantage point of any castle on the
western seaboard makes Eilean Donan and Loch Alsh one of Scotland's trademarks.

DUART CASTLE, MULL
The island's eastern "coast guard station" provides wonderful picture
opportunities from the Oban ferry; a simple, but evocative picture.

TROSSACHS KIRK
A photographer's dream; superb winter sunlight, superb location and not a tourist in sight!

CENTRAL REGION

DUMYAT

a difficult climb in bits but superb views west towards Abbey Craig and Stirling; south over the Links of Forth and east along the foothills of the Ochils; try it early morning.

DOLLAR

Castle Campbell taken from anywhere is dramatic (try to make the most of its location); the view of the town and the Cleish Hills from the golf course is lovely.

CRAIGFORTH

on the banks of the river just west of Stirling where the Teith flows into the Forth - two solitary trees make fantastic silhouettes for a sunset picture on a very quiet stretch of the water.

STIRLING CASTLE

best from the west but a great autumnal shot from the top of the golf course.

LOCHARD

at the east end a lochan greets you; surrounded by trees, with water lilies and reeds growing and a boat conveniently tied up to the jetty - if that wasn't enough, Ben Lomond is framed perfectly as the lochan exits to link up with big brother next door. Still one of my favourite pictures.

STRATHYRE

park at the Falls of Leny (two miles north of Callander) and take the stiff walk through the woods to the crags which have a superb view north west over Loch Lubnaig to Balqhuidder - early morning or late evening for best effect.

LOCH ACHRAY

the little church (Trossachs Kirk) sitting on the edge of Loch Achray just beyond Brig O'Turk makes for a classic composition with Ben Venue in the background - autumn or winter preferably. You might need to do a bit of wading to get the best shot!

TAYSIDE

FEE CORRIE

up Glen Clova (just one of the beautiful glens of Angus); park the car and take a two mile hike up into the amphitheatre of rock - a wonderful sight but extremely difficult to do justice with the camera.

LINTTRATHEN LOCH

near Alyth, this reservoir affords wonderful autumn shots - very still and colourful with some fishing boats if needed.!

GLEN ISLA

gorgeous in the autumn when the trees change; lovely pictures all the way up: try and frame Forter Castle against a backdrop of the hills to the north.

DUNKELD

another autumn visit required - autumn in Perthshire is something else - try the beech trees on the banks of the river Tay just west of the bridge; great shot of the Cathedral tower from the golf course (mornings only!)

CARNOUSTIE

the natural harbour made by the rocks at Westhaven and the colourful fishing boats guarantee some great shots - in the right light.

SPRING SUNSHINE, LOCH AWE
A cold April afternoon, lovely sunlight, a bare tree and of course,
Kilchurn Castle are the main ingredients of this different shot
of a much photographed Scottish landmark.

ST. ABBS HEAD
Early morning, St. Abbs Head. The reward for one hour's patience (while a band of cloud
cleared into the North Sea) was this lovely panorama of the clifftop rock and the village

GARDENSTOWN HARBOUR
Just one of the idyllic harbours along the north coast of Buchan. I wish I could be here for late summer sun on the houses and boats - that's the time of day, without a doubt.

GRAMPIAN

CAIRN O' MOUNT
> One of Scotland's classic views but not for the faint-hearted in winter time. Great westward views of Clachnaben and Mount Shade as you near Banchory.

BENNACHIE
> "Where the Gadie rins"; lovely views of the Don to the south, and Mither Tap is probably the favourite summit of the hill itself.

DUNNOTTAR CASTLE
> Take the coastal/cliff path around the bay to the south of the castle to see it in all its precarious splendour - early morning or evening for best effect.

VILLAGES OF THE NORTH COAST
> Take your pick from Crovie, Pennan, Gardenstown, Portsoy, Cullen, Portknockie, Findochty; gems of fishing havens on a 30 mile stretch of glorious coastline.

HIGHLANDS & ISLANDS

Impossible to list all the favourites, but don't miss out on

GLENCOE

Indescribable beauty, unbelievable atmosphere - no words really do it justice.

CASTLE STALKER

Off the Appin Coast - fabulous situation.

ARDNAMURCHAN

Bleak, bare, beautiful; views north to Rhum, Eigg and Skye are wonderful.

SOUTH MORAR

White sands and glorious views - and renowned for wonderful sunsets.

MULL

take at least two days to do justice to the bays, cliffs, beaches and villages; Tobermory, Dervaig, Calgary Bay, Torosay and Duart Castles; down the southern, twisting seaside road enjoy the lochs and islands; take an extra day for Iona and Staffa.

SKYE

Weather permitting, probably the most spectacular landscapes of the Western Isles; don't blink!

EILEAN DONAN CASTLE

Classic situation, but take the little road up the hill from Dornie for the view.

KINTAIL

Lovely and much - photographed from the high road above the southern shore of Loch Duich - worth every hairpin you meet.

PLOCKTON

Beautiful village which faces "the wrong way". Use the high ground on the Stromeferry road to do it justice.

TORRIDON AND APPLECROSS

see separate chapter.

INVERPOLLY AND ASSYNT

see separate chapter.

"THE BOOCHLE"
Autumn in Glencoe and a different shot of one of Glencoe's "sentries" - possibly its best known; a different shot again using the river and the lovely autumn colours around the bank to frame a wide-angle view of "The Great Shepherd".

LOCH AINORT AND BEINN DEARG
The north westerly members of the Cuillin family provide the perfect backdrop for this
morning shot of the sea-loch a few miles south of Sligachan.

LOCH NA KEAL, MULL
Bell heather and rocks feature strongly in the foreground of this shot
of one of Mull's many sealochs; Ben More and neighbours mistily
overlook the scene.

ROSEMOUNT, BLAIRGOWRIE
To me this picture epitomises golf in Scotland; elegant clubhouse, superb course and
heather in the foreground - a lovely composition.

OF AEROPLANES AND GOLF COURSES . . .

On the face of it, there is absolutely no connection between professional sprinting, motor dealing, aerial photography and golf. I shall now disprove that by recounting how those four diverse activities combined to provide me with opportunities to market my photographs in a manner which no planner could have remotely forecast.

Bob Swan, now Managing Director/owner of Kinghorn Garage in Fife, was, in his younger days, a professional sprinter. This pursuit took him, during the summer, to regular venues around the Highland Games circuit in Scotland, where he competed in front of enthusiastic audiences - and more than a few Scottish tourists.

I first became acquainted with Bob when we met at a golf dinner at Burntisland. He was, by this time in 1988, well established in the business, and I was delighted to be asked to take over accounting duties for him. We became friends, although he was visibly disappointed when I met him early in 1991 to tell him about my impending retiral from the practice.

Those feelings did not prevent him, however, from passing on a superb piece of advice on the possibility of marketing my photographs around the Games which he himself had so enjoyed. As a direct consequence, I therefore found myself at Inveraray and Luss Highland Games on consecutive days during Glasgow Fair fortnight in July 1992.

It was at Luss - a superb arena for such an event - that I first met Duncan Shand, and his delightful wife Jean and daughter Anna. They have become excellent customers, but a real bonus developed from our relationship in the summer of 1994, as a consequence of Duncan's job as an Air Traffic Controller at Prestwick.

On at least two occasions, he had offered me a trip in a plane to try some aerial photography. I had kept the offer very much in mind, but to be honest, until I felt I was in a better position with the sales of "ground level" landscapes, I dismissed the possibilities of aerial photographs as something purely for the future.

However, the staging of the 1994 Open Golf Championship at Turnberry, suddenly opened up a whole new ball game (sorry for the pun) especially as Duncan's work at Prestwick had led to him taking out membership of the local Flying Club, where he was a qualified pilot.

It dawned on me around May that I might take advantage of Duncan's offer of an aerial trip to see if the Ayrshire Coast - and Turnberry in particular - would produce quality photographs for me. Thereafter, I could attempt a marketing exercise in and around the village where many thousands would come for a week in July to enjoy Britain's greatest golf extravaganza.

As usual, it was all down to the weather. On this occasion, in addition to the best light (late afternoon/evening was ideal to catch the lowering sun on the Ayrshire coast) we needed calm aerial conditions. Even I had worked out that, difficult as it might be to take quality pictures from a small aircraft, it would be well nigh impossible if it was being blown around at the time!

We had a couple of false starts, weather-wise, before a series of telephone calls one Thursday resulted in a headlong dash from West Calder to Prestwick for a 5 pm take-off; the cloud breaks over the Firth of Clyde and increasing bursts of late May sunshine promised much. I was not disappointed.

I was terrified, however, I knew a Cessna was a "light" aircraft, but I wasn't aware you could push it with one hand! Somehow the piece of string I used to tie my window to the underside of the wing seemed totally appropriate; Duncan's confirmation that the plane was over twenty years old, but "they get safer as they get older" did not help my anxiety about dropping like a stone out of a clear blue sky onto Girvan beach.

Anyway, strapped in (not a lot of room to work in) and with camera at the ready, Duncan took us into the Ayrshire skies at around 5.30 pm. The light was super - I began to get excited.

An hour and a half later, we were taxi-ing to a halt again after a tremendous flight. I couldn't believe we had been airborne for so long; it felt like ten minutes. We had flown

RIVER TAY
Ancient and modern in the Firth of Tay; Broughty Castle and the Tay Bridges are the principal features of this aerial shot looking towards Dundee.

One of the successes from my first airborne adventure; the beautifully located Turnberry Hotel - with the new Spa alongside - and the village, lit by late evening sunshine.

NINTH TEE, TIGHNABRUAICH
Background reading again allowed me to find this tremendous location above the Kyles of
Bute; the arrival of an English visitor (complete with wonderful cricket sweater!) on the
ninth tee was pure coincidence. A great composition, superb views of the Kyles of Bute and
possibly the best picture I took on the Cowal peninsula.

CHAPTER IX

HOME OF GOLF
A different approach to The Old Course and one of the few occasions
on which I have used shallow depth of field with, for me anyway,
a highly satisfying outcome.

down to Turnberry, out to and around Ailsa Craig, back to the coast for a "double-take" of the golf courses, then took in Culzean Castle and Dunure on the return trip.

I had shot three rolls of film, but had found it very hard work. I had to twist in my seat to shoot backwards and downwards, and as soon as the camera lens was the slightest distance out of the window, it was struck by a 90 m.p.h. blast of air which threatened to blow it away.

As a result, faster film was required. I used 200 ASA and managed an aperture of F8 at 1/250th of a second. I hadn't a clue at the time how it would all turn out, but as it transpired, I finished up with 14 excellent shots from the trip, wasn't sick, and had a sense of expectation that I might just have something special for Turnberry.

I was right. Ten days later, Carol had made an appointment for me to present my photographs and cards to Jean Gamble from Girvan, who, in addition to owning a very successful business in the town, also held the franchise to run the gift shop in Turnberry Hotel.

For once, my timing was right. She liked the photographs, felt that both mounted prints and cards would sell in the shop, and finished up giving me the biggest order I had yet obtained in three years. I was absolutely thrilled, and a further order from "Present Company" in Maidens (next village northwards from Turnberry) simply put the icing on the cake.

Duncan Shand's involvement in all of this excitement cannot be overstated. It had been his idea, his interest in my work, and his skill at the controls which had allowed it all to happen.

Yet, he wasn't finished; an introduction to his colleague, Peter Malone, manager of Northfield Garage in Cowdenbeath, resulted in two further aerial adventures before the summer was out. Peter is, if anything, more fanatical about aeroplanes than Duncan. He had to be, because I twice had him at Edinburgh Airport at 6.00 am so that we could catch East Lothian and Fife coasts respectively in early morning sun.

Some thirty new pictures - one or two of the East Lothian area absolutely stunning - accrued from these trips. The Fife one was a bit traumatic, as fairly turbulent conditions over Elie found me but a mere fraction from violent airsickness. Fifteen minutes in higher altitude allowed the nausea to subside, however, and we got back down in one piece, with stomach intact. It had been touch and go.

At the time of writing, I have an eye on the 1995 Open at St. Andrews, and therefore plan another trip. I would love also to do the valley of the Tweed in autumn, and Perthshire in the same season.

Irrespective of what lies ahead as far as any aerial exploits are concerned, I simply cannot thank Duncan and Pete enough for their help and encouragement at a crucial stage in the development of the business. They have opened up a completely new market place for me - I hope I am able to take full advantage.

The capture of aerial photographs of the Turnberry, Gleneagles, Muirfield and Fife golf courses have helped to swell a growing number of photographs which I had begun to collect early in the new business.

While a great deal of quality landscape photography covers the remote, sparsely populated and wilder areas of Scotland, where the hand of man is not readily visible, I don't feel at all embarrassed at classing our golf courses and as equally important element.

Indeed, we possess the finest natural links courses in the world, where often one feels that golf was played first, and townships arrived second. The work of course designers has , I grant you, created man-made pleasures for Scotland's golfing hordes, but it has also given the photographer wonderful opportunities to use his skills to convey the atmosphere of Scottish golfing treasures to enthusiasts the world over.

Modern technology has given the greenkeeper the very best and latest equipment to make his own eighteen holes a most beautiful setting for the game. Over the last three years, I have been privileged to visit, walk upon and photograph many of them. Having last played golf seriously in the late 1970's, I cannot believe the improvements I have witnessed across the whole country as committees and councils have upgraded courses and clubhouses.

Scotland claims, deservedly, to be the "Home of Golf". The title does not sit lightly on those empowered to maintain that lofty position. Their efforts to produce, arguably, one of the greatest tourist attractions we possess, are absolutely magnificent, and I hope my camera can continue to do justice to their tees, fairways, bunkers and greens in times to come. Perhaps I might find more time for my own clubs to do them justice too?!

DALMAHOY
Having played the course often, I knew the shot I wanted; I also wanted early summer to catch the rhododendrons and I think the finished product justifies all the forethought.

DUNBAR HARBOUR
6 am in the morning, 900 feet up, low sun and the good old polariser all combine to
provide a dramatic aerial shot of old Dunbar harbour - plus the new swimming pool!

GOLF AND GORSE, MELROSE
An un-forecast glorious summer day in the Borders with the nine hole
course at Melrose and the Eildon Hills at their very best; the presence of
the ladies on the sixth green simply adds to the charm of the picture.

A FEW WORDS OF ADVICE

It is rare for a photographer to just happen upon the spectacular combination of the elements which will allow him to capture another dramatic Scottish landscape for his portfolio.

Occasionally, of course, Lady Luck smiles and he can fire away in a great location with stunning light on the scene - perhaps only for a few seconds - but that's enough to catch a classic for next year's calendars or publication in a magazine (see pages, for example).

By and large, however, the great majority of photographs of this amazing country are captured as a result of careful planning, months or years of built-up knowledge on sunrise and sunset times, scrutiny of weather forecasts, angles, locations, copious notes accumulated from other times - and, importantly, remembering failed compositions from a previous unsuccessful trip when the light has let one down.

Even the most careful planning, however, counts for nothing if the scene is not properly lit. Of all the aspects involved in quality landscape photography, this is the most crucial.

Carefully planned expeditions to Scottish locations which I have wished to add to my portfolio have all too often yielded nothing of exhibitable quality simply because the light killed any opportunities. I think particularly of Appin (Castle Stalker), Lower Largo (see chapter II), Turnberry, Culzean and Ayr (trips 1 *and* 2!) Loch an Eilein (near Aviemore) and the Spey Valley, and a growing number of others; my chapter on Torridon says it all.

It is useful, of course, just to be there and to find preferred views and compositions which can be placed in the memory bank and save a lot of time on the next visit. But it is frustrating to drive 150 miles and find yourself under flat grey cloud which hadn't merited even a passing mention on weather forecasts of the preceding days.

For the amateur landscape photographer, of course, the disappointment of not seeing his holiday view in the right circumstances to capture it on film can be even more depressing. At least I have the opportunity of a second, or even third visit; the holiday maker may only have one chance, and that is a shame.

Anyway, assuming you are lucky, how should you go about ensuring that you see the chance when it comes and that your holiday shots turn out the way you would wish? I think we probably have to divide you into two categories - and I don't mean any offence - and look at advising each from a different perspective.

First, the "Happy Snapper". He or she will have a little compact camera, or a fifteen-year-old job which has bruises and scratches having fought its way through the Costa Brava, Blackpool or Saltcoats in the rain; both are amply capable of producing excellent results with a little thought and patience, but 'Happy Snappers' generally have little of these attributes. (My wife falls unashamedly into this category. She has no patience, and despite possessing some excellent artistic skills, wishes nothing more than to wind the car window down, lean out, take aim and fire; if you recognise these symptoms, Part One is for you!).

Second, the keen amateur, who will certainly have better (and more adaptable) equipment, possibly a couple of lenses for his or her 35mm SLR (Single Lens Reflex) camera, or very probably nowadays an all-singing-and-dancing fully automatic machine which does everything apart from parting the clouds at the right moment.

The qualities which all leading 35mm manufacturers now display in the vast array of models available to the general public actually make poor picture taking quite difficult. They do, however, make creative picture taking hard since the photographer becomes lazy and allows the camera to decide itself how to meter, and then execute the shot. The more experienced amateur, however, will not become a slave to the automation and will use the other functions on the camera to create his own pictures. The more thought and time you take, the better the results - promise!

PART 1 - THE HAPPY SNAPPER

1

Don't pick any old film for your camera. Use 200 ASA film for reasonable light (summertime/snow scenes/the beach etc.) and faster 400ASA film for poor light (winter, moody cloud scenes, dull weather etc).

2

Don't just leap out of the car or off the coach into the nearest layby and fire away. You are guaranteed to include a wastepaper basket, telegraph pole or the bus driver's left arm in the picture. Look at your proposed view carefully, and try to exclude unwanted objects or people.

3

Don't be a slave to the "view" or "landscape" shape of your camera's normal holding position. Turn the camera through 90 degrees and see if the scene looks better (if you are looking for a nice shot of Auntie Beannie against the backdrop of a Glencoe mountain, you will lose her legs and probably her head unless you think about "upright" or "portrait" shape).

4

Fill up the composition with your main subject, whether it be Auntie Beannie or Glencoe. Try to place the main subject in a position which will catch the viewer's attention, and don't include stuff that does not contribute to the shot (waste paper, wires, lampposts, nasty little boys etc. etc.!). Try, if possible, not to plant your main feature in the middle of the picture (whether that be vertical or horizontal). Ideally use a division of the view into thirds, rather than halves, and make that your rule of thumb.

5

Don't follow the crowd, sheep-like, to take your picture. By moving only a few yards - up, down, forward or back - or by crouching, or by standing on something, you can create a much better composition. It is amazing how many different shots you can take within an area of only a few cubic feet.

6

Don't, once exposed,allow your film to sit in 90 degrees of heat in the back seat of the car. Keep it cool if possible and take it for processing as soon as you can.

INVERNESS
Springtime by the banks of the Ness, and a nice composition provides the ideal opportunity in excellent light. Unfortunately, I couldn't hide the road sign!

HIGHLIGHTS
Looking for a different composition in Edinburgh after dark, the 400 lens picks out the Bank of Scotland and the Castle and almost creates three pictures in one.

7

With the greatest of respect to High Street outlets, who now advertise cut-price processing and printing offers, bear in mind that the cheaper the processing cost the more likely it is that your machine-produced prints may disappoint. Try to use an outlet which has a proven track record of reasonable quality.

8

If you are unhappy with your final prints, don't despair. Check the negatives. If they are good and 'strong' go back to the shop and politely ask for a set of reprints (the machine settings in a modern photolab can, within a very small range, produce vastly different colour densities and balance).

9

Learn from your mistakes by studying the prints and remembering where you went wrong on last year's holiday. Then put the lessons you have learned to good use.

PART 2 - THE ENTHUSIASTIC AMATEUR

1

Read the aforementioned list on the 'Happy Snapper'. If you can honestly conclude that your picture-making abilities have graduated from that level, read on. Irrespective - check the list again so that these ***basic rules are firmly implanted in your mind.***

2

Quality landscape photography is impossible without ***using a tripod.*** It is, undoubtedly, the most important accessory of my entire equipment. In poor light, or with slow film (100 ASA or less) the absolute immobility of your camera is essential.

3

The perennial problem - choice of film

a

Prints or transparencies? Despite what you may have read or been told, you will never be one hundred per cent happy with prints produced from transparency film. I myself have often been frustrated that a super transparency shot on Fuji Velvia (or RDP 120 in Medium Format) has simply not translated into a quality 12 x 8 print, my most requested size. Thus, if you want a permanent record on your wall of a favourite shot, use negative, rather than reversal film. Incidentally, it is not well known that highly acceptable transparencies can be produced from negatives, so why not try 'the other way round' and see what happens - perhaps the best of both worlds?

b

Film Speed; - I have experimented with speeds from 25 ASA to 400 ASA. The lowest, in Scotland at any rate, has proved very frustrating as in poor light, or with a view which will produce a predominantly moody picture, exposure time may have to be as much as two or three seconds. If, therefore, there is any movement in your composition (water, trees etc.) the finished article could be unacceptable. I have happily settled for Fuji's Reala film which at 100 ASA has wonderfully fine grain and extremely natural colour rendition. I have also, on occasion, been as much as two stops outwith the correct exposure and yet a highly acceptable print has still been obtained. For me, it is unbeatable.

Nevertheless if your photography of the outdoors will essentially involve movement (sports, mountaineering etc.) you should manage to 'freeze' the more sedate of those at 200 ASA, but go up to 400 ASA for faster subjects.

4

To obtain the sharpest possible results, and maximum depth- of- field in your shots, you need to use the *smallest aperture* you can (bigger F number) and therefore exposure times (the length of time over which the shutter will remain open) will be longer. I normally find that, early or late in the day, I need a quarter or an eighth of a second at F22 using 100 ASA film.

5

Plan your photography. It is unlikely that you will take consistently breathtaking photographs by enjoying - just when you need them - a succession of bursts of glorious sun against black thundery skies or the like. Further, unless you have researched your locations either by previous visits, by map reading, checking tide times etc. or by studying books on the area, you might well arrive at the wrong time of day. Finally, it goes without saying that you cannot study enough weather forecasts - perhaps from three or four days in advance of your visit. The good landscape photographer doesn't want bright midday sun, but he does want the

STIRLING BRIG'
One of these days when the "I'll take the camera just in case" afterthought reaped rich rewards. A tremendous storm over Stirling had moved over to Abbey Craig and a convenient burst of sun hit the Brig at precisely the right moment. Very proud of this shot - it is extremely difficult to compose as so much modernistic gunge is all around.

CHAPTER X

LUNAN BAY
Bag nets at Lunan Bay, near Montrose, captured in silhouette against an early morning burst of sun; graduated grey filter the essential accessory!

best or most dramatic early morning or late evening light to allow him the chance to capture the most characterful and detailed images.

6

If you are not a darkroom enthusiast, be prepared to spend a bit more on processing and printing being done by a *quality laboratory* The extra revenue I have enjoyed as a result of the help which I have had from Gordon Pruce, Bruce Hutcheon and their team at Ideal Format in Edinburgh has been incalculable. From suggestions on use of film, to little manipulations of colour balance or density on my prints, to consistent production, time after time, of high quality photographs (from the tiniest at 3" x 2". to the largest at 48" x 36") their service has been quite superb. It has not happened by accident. They are thoroughly good professionals who have gone out of their way to develop a relationship with their customers and thus familiarised themselves with the end product which the photographer is always seeking. Remember that High Street processing will do no more than run your negatives through a machine with little or no 'hands-on' adjustment to colour balance or density. You will therefore get back what you pay for, acceptable as many of these may be. For the best and most professional results, be prepared to spend that bit more for greater quality.

7

Be careful with your use of filtration. Skylight or ultraviolet filters should never be off the lenses, and these will ensure that the blue cast which is in the atmosphere but invisible to the naked eye is not reproduced on your final prints. I make extensive use of polarising filters which are wonderful for deepening colours, cutting down reflections and reducing haze, and if you happen to catch a composition where you are at exactly right angles to the rays from the sun, the effect of the polariser is quite stunning. Beyond that, however, the only other filter which I use to any great degree is the grey graduated filter; at times of high contrast between, for example, bright sun and dark subject matter, the grey grad. is invaluable and is the only means possible of getting some detail into your foreground when the sun or sky is so bright. There are hundreds of other filters available, but I find that they take the natural effect of the scene away and my advice would be to use them sparingly, if at all.

8

Be patient. Only occasionally have I arrived at a location, taken a few pictures which were just what I was looking for, and been off again within a few minutes. Landscape photography of high quality just doesn't work like that. For an hour and a half early one morning I stood atop the cliffs on St Abbs' Head, waiting for a stubborn band of grey cloud to clear the sun. Twice I have climbed Conic Hill, above Balmaha on Loch Lomond (forty five minutes of difficult climbing on predominantly steep slopes). On the first occasion, the sky - late afternoon - was cloudless, and I waited for two hours for a low dramatic sunset. It never came; the sun went down, pale yellow and quite unsympathetic towards my desires for colourful reflections on the still water of the loch. But, better luck next time - my patience was rewarded with a cracking afterglow behind the Arrochar Alps, and then some lovely contrast on the surface of the water produced three cracking pictures. The message is clear - be patient!

Of course, you need some luck, and I would like to think that the misfortunes and frustrations of long journeys for nothing have been compensated by unexpected bonuses on other days. However the element of chance should be relegated to the very bottom of any list of key factors in successful landscape photography. Prepare yourself as well as you possibly can, then keep your fingers crossed that all the planning is rewarded by the conditions you wanted - and expected.

ST. MONANS
Despite the quality of the sunshine, it wasn't time for refloating the boats after another winter. That fact allowed me to frame the harbour-side houses and so capture a different view of this much photographed East Neuk of Fife village.

A LOOK INTO THE CRYSTAL BALL

You do not require to be a potential Brain of Britain to know just how fast technology is changing our world. If someone had said to me twenty years ago that we would soon be able to sit in our living rooms, pump in a few numbers on a television key pad and order our shopping, I know what I would have said to them. Therefore any forecast of future developments in photography is fraught with the greatest difficulty. However, informed sources (Gordon Pruce on one hand and John Grayson of Fuji Film (U.K.) Ltd. on the other) tell me to expect the following:-

The basic camera , which has undergone many fundamental changes in the last ten years or so, will not continue the revolution quite so dramatically. There will, however, be more advances in the use of electronics. For example, at the time of writing , Fuji, in conjunction with Nikon, have produced a 35mm disk camera linked, if desired, straight into a computer. No film is needed, the image being held on disk, and , having manipulated the picture on-screen if required, prints can then be made.

Developments there will obviously be (with Japan still leading the way) but the rapid evolution of computer - aided cameras should start to slow down.

As far as film is concerned, improvements are taking place all the time, particularly in the structure of the emulsion, and the use of finer and finer grain. Gordon now anticipates new developments every eighteenth months or so, but interestingly observes that, despite the arrival of electronic imaging, film reproduction is still unbeatable for quality.

Amateur photographers may therefore breathe easy, as the best possible film for your cameras will remain available for a long time to come, and in the general high qualities that you have enjoyed in recent years. Fuji and Agfa, in particular, continue research and development space, and that would indicate that, irrespective of technological wizardry in other directions, basic film production remains assured.

There have been , as I have already remarked, dramatic developments in photography over the last ten years or so, and the pace of change is bound to slow, in Gordon's opinion. If, for example, photography becomes even more dependant on electronics, and perhaps automation, then problems of flat batteries - not to mention rising costs of these - may well limit the progress of manufacturers. It's an interesting position, and as it will always be risky, particularly in difficult lighting situations, to rely totally on metering "through the lens", some degree of manual picture - taking is always going to be necessary, in my opinion.

Recently, we have witnessed the advent of photographic compact discs. While this has been an intriguing development, the concept has by no means taken off; it may be that, like refrigeration in the early 1960's the market place has not yet seen the wisdom of wholesale investment in the idea. At any rate, there is still ample demand for run-of-the-mill, good old fashioned photograph albums and slide shows so someone isn't convinced that CD is the way ahead!

On another aspect, equipment is now available which allows the photographer to take still pictures from his home video. It currently costs around six to seven hundred pounds, but the obvious question arises: - why not use a still camera in the first place? We are not at all convinced that clever advertising or promotional literature on exciting photographic developments will hood-wink the camera enthusiast into ditching his traditional and proven equipment; not yet, anyway!

As far as technological progress will affect our professional photographic laboratories, Gordon points out that the like of Fuji and Agfa are continuing to devote substantial investment to the research and development of traditional processing and printing methods, the indication therefore being that these two companies, at least, still see the immediate future of photography requiring accepted laboratory techniques.

Despite the steady reduction in costs which has generally accompanied the 'ageing' of new equipment, laboratory machinery and fittings are still extremely expensive, so cost limitations for many independent labs still prohibit swift replacement of traditional methods.

Perhaps the market place is not quite ready for further revolutions in technology? What is the point, for example, in investing, say £30000 in a brand new Minilab when only a year later an updated model is available at £20000?

It is worrying that the very latest machine off a production line can so quickly be superseded by another, but the fact that modern technology is creating this syndrome is perhaps also making it its own worst enemy. Time will tell.

For the moment, rest easy that ample quality exists in your professional laboratory to reproduce, even more accurately and sharply, the films which you hand in for processing. It does appear that the continuation of improvements in emulsion quality, first, and laboratory equipment, second, will guarantee you the very best possible results from your picture taking. Provided, that is, you have created good pictures yourself!

On a personal note, how do I see things developing over the next few years? Touching wood, I seem to have the business on a reasonably firm base and I hope I can build on that in the immediate future. I have no wish to be a millionaire but I would like to think within the next couple of years, that profits would be sufficient to allow me to continue an upgrade of my equipment, keep wolves from the door, tuck away a reasonable pension contribution for the future and continue to enjoy a few weeks' holiday at our beloved La Manga.

Of most immediate concern, I required to find premises from which to operate the business. Two rooms in our house were previously fully taken up as office and store, a third was beginning to head that way, and there was no more room in the outhouses for anything.

It was essential, of course, that I begin the business from home to see if it would become established in the market place; there was absolutely no point in incurring what would have been crippling establishment costs in some High Street location somewhere when I had no idea in the early days whether there was a future or not.

However, premises which would double up as a gallery opening on to a main street, with additional space for the greeting card side of things to be accommodated (workshop/store/office), really became a priority in 1994.

The vast majority of my product is, of course, tourist related and the ideal location required the expectation of a steady through- put of visitors or tourists, and if possible have a reasonably sized population to maintain a decent level of turnover at either end of the tourist season.

Linlithgow and South Queensferry both came into the aforementioned categories and, with a pretty solid customer base in my home town of Linlithgow, it would have been first choice. The right property there, however, was very hard to find and demanded a price which I just could not afford. For exactly these reasons, an interest had to be shelved in such premises in the Autumn of 1994.

I could seriously embarrass a certain official of Edinburgh District Council for leading me horrendously up the garden path over an ideal property in South Queensferry in the earlier part of 1994, but I will spare his blushes.

A good Edinburgh location of course would also have been ideal, but the thought of attempting to commute regularly to a city whose accessibility over the last ten or fifteen years has, slowly but surely, been strangled by the short comings of a non-existent transport policy filled me with horror. Edinburgh's inner city is choking, and if the trickle of City Centre stores to new out-of-town locations should become a flood - which is more than likely - then the potential customers who currently throng Princes Street and its surrounds will not be there anyway.

As Micawber (I think!) once said, however, "Something always turns up". At the time of writing, I have had an offer accepted for a high street property in South Queensferry. Although a huge amount of work requires to be done before the gallery doors can be open to the public, I feel excited at all the possibilities surrounding the development. By the time this book reaches the reader, I hope the till might be jangling!

On a more positive note, I sincerely hope that I can continue to expand the portfolio of Scottish pictures. In 1994, I virtually doubled the number of exhibits. Despite that, I am still regularly asked if I have shots of parts of the country which I have not yet visited. It is one of the great frustrations that potential custom is lost because, being relatively late into the photography of the landscape, I have not yet had the time to build a portfolio which remotely resembles that of many of our top Scottish photographers.

Nevertheless, in the foreseeable future, I hope I will be able to strike from the list on the board in my office (under section 'locations requested') the following;-

GLEN AAFFRIC, EATER ROSS, KINLOCHBERVIE AND DURNESS AREAS, THE OUTER HEBRIDES, ISLAY, IONA, KINTYRE, THE SPEY VALLEY, nearer home, if by the time you are reading this chapter I have not presented a certain lady with pictures of Bo'ness I will be in real trouble!

It will be a long time before that list is all 'in the can' and it is much too simplistic to believe that, on my first visit, I will get the shots I'm looking for. Nevertheless, the planning of the trip and the excitement which I inevitably feel when I reach a previously unexplored part of Scotland will be impossible to suppress.

Scotland has that kind of effect on you and if you don't have that feeling, then the offerings of the finest landscape in the world are simply not for you.

They are for me, and I have no doubt that it will ever be thus. Hard as it is in this beautiful country, I constantly strive to capture the changing moods, atmosphere and light to pass on to the viewer. There have been, and there will be in the future, occasions when I find this an impossibility. It is at such a time that you realise, in conceding defeat, that Scotland's landscape controls the photographer. No matter the swift oncoming of technological miracles, the camera will never control the amazing co-existence of hills, mountains, glens, shores and islands which are Scotland.

LOCH NA-H'ACHLAISE
November in the black mount, on the west edge of Rannoch Moor; a lovely composition looking towards the Munros around Glen Etive.

WITH THANKS TO......

In the early days of any new small business, a sole trader inevitably has to do everything. In my case, that meant taking photographs, organising their presentation, trying to market them, selling them, and, if that wasn't enough, doing all the administration, book keeping, letter writing, telephoning etc.

W hen it becomes established, however, he must invest in other people to help, without whom he will soon be "physically over-trading" (to use a phrase which I coined from my accounting days) and soon he could be heading for problems.

It is essential therefore that the development of the small business finds the owner released to continue the things he is best at, while he produces a team around him to take on those aspects which he has to delegate.

In getting my business off the ground, exactly these circumstances have pertained, although some of my "team" have been on board from the very start. I make no apologies, however, for now acknowledging the assistance which I have had from a variety of sources, without which I probably wouldn't have even reached first base!

The service provided by my photographic laboratory, IDEAL FORMAT LTD., from Leith, has played a huge part in the success of the business to date.

I cannot over-emphasise the wealth of advice, encouragement and moral support which they have given me over the crucial early years. Never too busy for a chat, always ready with a suggestion, ever willing to lend equipment, and problem-solver supreme, GORDON PRUCE's wealth of experience, both as a photographer and a top photo-lab professional must make him one of the best in the country.

SHEENA HUNTLY, of "EYE LEVEL" in Laurieston, fulfilled all early mounting and framing needs of the business and her service was excellent.

If Sheena's work in the early days was invaluable, then it is hard to find the right adjective to describe the input of PHILIP KERNOHAN of "EMMA K", from Balerno. He set up his own embroidery and framing business in 1992 with his wife EMMA. As time has gone on, his ability to see colours in my pictures and find complementary mounts and frames has been uncanny. The tremendous service which he has provided, and the advice which he has gladly offered when needed has again been invaluable.

My attempts at marketing the business were not disastrous, but were certainly, in part, misdirected. The same cannot be said for the advertising, design and creative help I have received from COLIN and MARION MCLAREN, co-Directors of EDMONDS ADVERTISING LTD. in Leith.

The new brochure which Edmonds produced for me in 1993 was of the very highest quality and has been much admired both by customers and fellow traders, and on the advertising side, Marion has been equally helpful.

A growing list of photographs requires to be properly logged and updated. It was Colin's suggestion that I should computerise them, and LEIGH HAILSTONES, one of Edmonds' administration team, painstakingly logged around 500 titles for me to set up a computerised portfolio. Since then, despite my bad writing and sometimes ineligible picture titles, she has regularly kept the list up to date for me and I must thank her too for all her help and patience.

Before moving on, it would be remiss of me not to mention the efforts of the whole team at Edmonds in producing this very book. Of course, it is a milestone in my career, but it is also such for Edmonds.

If those aforementioned in this list have been key players I have to say that help and advice from lots of others has not been hard to find. In no particular order, and hopefully without causing offence, the following have all contributed in one way or another and deserve their mention.

BARRY ANDERSON gave me my chance at PASTIME PUBLICATIONS (as you will see from an earlier chapter), and I have to thank him for giving me the opportunity to get a foot on the ladder of "Scotland - Home of Golf". More recently TERRY CLARK has taken over and he has already made his mark with an invitation to me to produce the English Golf Handbook.

CHAPTER XII

COLIN and ALISON PARVIN, a delightful couple who are managers of the HAWES INN at South Queensferry, organised accommodation for my South Queensferry exhibitions, and I must pass on thanks for their help and involvement. Hopefully with a base established in the town I will see more of them now!

KIM WIGHTMAN, who with her husband SAM, now run the highly successful CAFE JARDIN, just off the A90 at Kinross, has exhibited my framed pictures in the restaurant for some three years. Such is never a dripping roast, but the publicity through displaying my pictures in quality establishments like this should not be underestimated and it was nice of them to think of me first.

Similar comments apply to MARGARET WARDROP, (whose "ELLIOT INTERIORS" in Linlithgow High Street has brought her deserved rewards for the courage to open a capital-sapping furniture outlet) and to the BEECRAIGS RESTAURANT, beautifully situated in the hills between Linlithgow and Bathgate. They have displayed my pictures for some two years. Sales have been steady, if not spectacular, but the chance to have local photographs displayed is invaluable, and I thank MARGARET and JOYCE MCGURK for all they have done to help.

MIKE WHEATLEY has been a friend of mine for years. We met on the cricket field, struck up a friendship when he came to the Linlithgow area in the 1970's, and that friendship blossomed to the extent that he was best man at our wedding in 1989. His delightful wife ANNE, and daughters ANGELA and JENNY, have regularly appeared at my shows and have helped the physical dismantling of a huge number of exhibits, packing and carting of heavy boxes up and downstairs in pitch darkness. It would be completely wrong if they were to be omitted from any list of "thank yous".

I can vividly recall the Sunday lunchtime early in 1991 when, as usual, I'd had a Sunday day out with CAMPBELL and ALISTAIR. Before the customary weekly game of snooker, we headed for Fife and a lunch in Falkland. It was there that I told them I was packing up my practice and embarking on a new and risky photographic career. Campbell has never been slow to express his thoughts, and therefore it was with some trepidation that I awaited a reaction. It was nothing but supportive, from both of them, and in the early days they willingly assisted at the exhibitions and shows around Central Scotland - many of which, as you will read, were non-productive and must have bored them to tears, but I needed support from all the family in the early days and it was not long in coming.

My stepson, LEE, while less available for physical help, has been there when it mattered. Despite a near-disaster when precious slides from a long trip to England were in the boot of his car and almost destroyed by squashed tomatoes, his help and advice on the artistic side of things has been greatly appreciated. He is now close to the end of a four year Interior Design course at Telford College and I hope his career is just reward for the natural artistic and design skills which he possesses. To all the boys, therefore, I offer thanks for help and support at a crucial time.

I have deliberately left the best till last. Without the support, encouragement, criticism and unpaid instruction from CAROL, I simply would not have made it this far. Her advice on marketing and selling techniques and patient criticism of thousands of photographs is priceless. (Her forbearance of 3am awakenings with rattling drawers, stubbed toes in the darkness on bedroom tables, or hiss of shell-suit bottoms has been something else!).

Scorpios are pioneers, go-getters and are fired with a passion to succeed. In 1992 and 1993, I had to fight hard to avoid failure. Always, however, despite serious doubts which I knew she had about my ever making a success of the new business ("you said you'd give it a year - it's two years now and you're still not making any money" was a typical observation) she was the first to admire new photographs, or feel good that a potential sale had been achieved, or offer a bit of advice when it was needed.

There were other occasions (especially at a difficult time in her own life and business career) when she could have seen it all far enough. Whole weekends away at shows, particularly in the summer outdoor event season took their toll on the togetherness which we had never failed to appreciate and enjoy. There was a point when our entire relationship was under threat as a result of it all. Gradually, having talked it out, we recovered lost ground, and now, happily (I think!) we are each enjoying our individual careers and at the same time have rebuilt the closeness which has always been such an important factor in our lives together. We were discussing the possibilities around a big calendar for 1994, when her seemingly innocent remark "why don't you do it all in book form?" spawned the whole idea of this short autobiography. Thus I find myself in the final chapter, perhaps a year after that suggestion was floated.

I'm sure Carol wishes now that she had kept her big mouth shut, because she was landed with the huge task of typing out the script. Happily, that has coincided with the arrival of her new computer and to some degree at least, I'm sure she has enjoyed playing around with the latest technology from Apple MacIntosh. Thank goodness for the "spell check" facility. It has been a Godsend - she is not the world's greatest speller!

To say "thank you" for all she has done in the last three or four years seems totally inadequate and I know in her own shy, unassuming fashion (!) she will resent this public expression of my gratitude. It needed to be said, however, so let it be so.

Finally, I have to thank hundreds and perhaps thousands of customers, both private and trade, who, by purchasing a card, a calendar, a picture or even a copy of this book have allowed me to continue the enjoyment of the Scottish landscape. It is still hard to believe all that has happened since that fateful April day in 1991, but I will never have any regrets at the abandonment of a career which for reasons outwith my control, was about to go haywire.

Rather I will continue to marvel at the opportunity presented to me, which has allowed me to see and capture the glories of this amazing place and to look forward to a multitude of new surprises which await further trips around Scotland.

The final expression of gratitude must therefore go to MOTHER NATURE, and to her ancient, long-gone army of sculptors and excavators who have created the glorious masterpiece of the Scottish landscape.

Tantallon Castle
The dramatic location of Tantallon Castle is never better in evidence than 'from the air' the erratic curves and cliffs of the East Lothian coastline finish the composition off nicely.

MY CURRENT LIST OF EQUIPMENT

35 MM
Minolta 7000 AF bodies - 2
Minolta 28mm wide angle lens*
Minolta 50mm Standard lens*
Minolta 70-210mm zoom lens*
Minolta 50mm macro lens (close up)
Sigma 400mm telephoto lens*
Minolta 2800 AF programmed flash gun
Minolta flash adaptor & cable
Minolta remote control shutter release cable
Cobra Profile tripod
Polarising filter (circular) for each size of lens
Cokin filter adaptor/holder for each size of lens
Cokin graduated filters; grey, blue, tobacco, pink (sunset)

*Ultra - Violet filter permanently fitted.

FILM USED
100 ASA (currently Fuji Reala) for prints
50 ASA (currently Fuji Provia) for transparencies
125 ASA (currently Agfa Optima) for poorer light
400 ASA (currently Fuji) for aerial photography

SPECIAL CLOTHING
Climbing boots/socks
Oilskins
Waterproof bottoms
Thermal underwear

MEDIUM FORMAT
Mamiya 645 body with cd prism
Mamiya 50mm wide angle lens*
Mamiya 80mm Standard lens*
Mamiya 150mm telephoto lens*
Mamiya motor drive
shutter release cable
Polarising filter for each size of lens
Manfrotto 055C tripod

FILM USED
100 ASA (currently Fuji Reala NSP 120) for prints
100 ASA (currently Fuji Provia RSP 120) for transparencies

*Ultra - Violet filter permanently fitted.

OTHER ACCESSORIES CARRIED
Exposure meter
Pads & Pens
Spirit level (adapted to fit hot shoe of flash holder)
Lens fluid/cleaning cloth/tissues
Length of cord
Spare batteries (2 sets)
Insect repellent
Pair of ladies' gloves (for cold weather camera operating)
Polythene bag (camera cover in rain)
Compass